STRATEGIES OF POLITICAL INQUIRY

SAGE FOCUS EDITIONS

Strategies of Political Inquiry

Edited by
Elinor Ostrom

SAGE PUBLICATIONS
Beverly Hills / London / New Delhi

For information address:

SAGE Publications, Inc.
275 South Beverly Drive
Beverly Hills, California 90212

SAGE Publications India Pvt. Ltd.
C-236 Defence Colony
New Delhi 110 024, India

SAGE Publications Ltd
28 Banner Street
London EC1Y 8QE, England

Printed in the United States of America

Library of Congress Cataloging in Publication Data

Main entry under title:

Strategies of political inquiry.

(Sage focus editions; 48)
Bibliography: p.
Contents: Beyond positivism / Elinor Ostrom—On getting from here to there / G. R. Boynton—The histor-ical nature of social-scientific knowledge / Roger Benjamin—[etc.]
    1. Political science—Addresses, essays, lectures.
2. Political science—Research—Addresses, essays, lectures. I. Ostrom, Elinor
JA71.S793   320'.072   82-852
ISBN 0-8039-1817-8   AACR2
ISBN 0-8039-1818-6 (pbk.)

FIRST PRINTING

pd
4-22-83

STRATEGIES OF POLITICAL INQUIRY

CONTENTS

Preface

Besides the central themes that unite the chapters brought together in this volume, all of the chapters were presented to colleagues in the Department of Political Science at Indiana University during the course of the past several years. During the academic year 1978-1979, G. R. Boynton spent a year working with Dina Zinnes and John Gillespie at the Center for International Policy Studies on a research project funded by the National Science Foundation (Grant SPI 78-19060). During the course of that year he made several presentations at different colloquia at CIPS, at the Workshop in Political Theory and Policy Analysis, and the Department of Political Science. The paper, "Getting from Here to There," which is Chapter 2 of this book, was written during that academic year.

During the spring of 1980, Professor John Sprague of the Department of Political Science at Washington University visited the campus and gave a methodology workshop lecture for the Political Science Data Lab on "Is There a Micro-Theory Consistent with Contextual Analysis?" which he later wrote for inclusion in this volume.

During the 1980-1981 academic year, the Department of Political Science was able, through the help of the College of Arts and Sciences at Indiana University, to establish a Distinguished Lecture Series. During the course of that year, lectures were presented by J. Donald Moon on October 9, 1980; Roger Benjamin on March 5, 1981; and Brian Barry on April 23, 1981. We are appreciative of the funding made available by the College of Arts and Sciences for this lecture series.

Larry Kiser of the Center for Social and Economic Research at Eastern Washington University was a postdoctoral trainee at

the Workshop in Political Theory and Policy Analysis for the
two-year period from 1978 through 1980. During that time, he
and Elinor Ostrom began a monograph-length manuscript on
the three worlds of political economy models. The last chapter
in this volume provides an overview of that manuscript.

1

Beyond Positivism

An Introduction to This Volume

ELINOR OSTROM

Some intellectual eras come to an end with a bang. Others end with a whimper. Those that end suddenly are swept out by the rapid acceptance of a new theory or a major finding that makes the continuation of old beliefs impossible. Most intellectual eras in the social sciences may end with a whimper—with a vague sense of unease that not much progress has been made for all the efforts of able and hardworking scholars. My personal sense is that we are coming to an end of an era in political science, a slow, whimpering end.

The signs of the demise of an old era include a level of disquietude among the practitioners of a discipline. This volume contains essays written by some of the more able practicing empirical theorists in the country. Most of them indicate some dissatisfaction with the current status of political science. Boynton (Chapter 2) is concerned that the "most glaring weakness in our program has been the discontinuity between theory and research." Moon (Chapter 6) indicates that "one of the major shortcomings or problems of political science is the apparent confusion and diversity of standards in our field." Benjamin

(Chapter 3) argues that "as soon as we begin to achieve some success in apprehending an important political process, diachronic change occurs in such fields as modernization to render our models obsolete."

Signs of dissatisfaction with the discipline are not new, however. Since World War II major confrontations have occurred within political science. Some have occurred in the literature (MacIntyre, 1967; Winch, 1958; Feyerabend, 1970; Falco, 1973; Goldberg, 1963; Laslett et al., 1972).

However, many of the arguments have been fought as departments made recruitment and curricular decisions. The "quantitative versus nonquantitative" dispute has surfaced in many departments each time a new faculty member is hired as colleagues debate about the appropriateness of the approach taken by candidates. Designing undergraduate or graduate curricula is another process likely to invoke a similar conflict. Those taking the antiquantitative position have argued that studying relationships using quantitative data does not provide an adequate understanding of the political world. Advocates of a more quantitative approach to political science have argued that without careful measurement and the use of analytic techniques, one does not have a basis for knowing anything. In some subdisciplines of political science, specialized fields of inquiry have been identified by their stance in the quantitative versus nonquantitative dispute—quantitative international relations is one example.

While strong feelings have been triggered, the quantitative versus nonquantitative dispute did not generally touch fundamental issues of importance to understanding political phenomena. When couched as a fight between those who quantify and those who do not, the dispute does not touch the central question of what are the basic processes occurring in different political systems in different eras. Rather, the dispute has centered on the way variables are coded and the type of statistics used as criteria to establish that a relationship between one variable and a second variable exists. It has been, to a large extent, an intellectual confrontation over how to represent descriptions of the world, rather than an argument about different organizing principles for understanding the world. Both camps have remained fundamentally descriptive in their approach to the study of political phenomena.

The disquietude reflected in the essays in this volume differs from the discontent articulated by those scholars pushing for a more quantitative approach to political science. The concern here is that after several decades of far more rigorous empirical research, the hoped for cumulation of knowledge into a coherent body of theory has not occurred. This is a lament from those who have been, as Boynton phrases it, "in the research camp."

The central theme of the essays in this volume is the need for the development of theory as the basis of our discipline. Benjamin (Chapter 3) concludes after assessing the state of comparative political inquiry that "we should be concerned again with opening up new concepts, reworking old questions, developing new puzzles, junking old theories and developing new ones, rather than developing and applying methodologies." While political scientists have been asserting that theory should be the basis of our discipline throughout the postwar era, the definition of what constitutes proper theory is used differently here from the definition of theory articulated by logical positivists and accepted by many scholars in the discipline.

To some extent the heavy emphasis on descriptive, empirical, quantitative work may have resulted from the naive acceptance of a particular school of philosophy of science. The books that had the most influence on our conception of what theory should be were for many years those by Brodbeck (1968), Hempel (1965), Nagel (1961), and Rudner (1966). At the time these authors accepted the logical positivist position on the type of scientific method to form the foundation of the social sciences. In a critique of rational choice theories from a covering law perspective, Terry Moe (1979: 216) aptly describes the central belief system of the logical positivist's approach.

> There is a fundamental unity of scientific method across the natural and social sciences; in both, the purpose of science is the explanation

of events and the nature of explanation is nomological. An event is explained when a statement of its . . . occurrence is deductively subsumed under lawlike statements and statements of initial conditions; and these logically prior statements, the theoretical premises, must be well-confirmed by the available evidence, since it is the presumed truth of the premises that logically justifies the expectation of the event's occurrence. Scientific progress hinges on the discovery of well-confirmed lawlike statements and on their integration into increasingly general and comprehensive theoretical structures.[1]

If in order to have a theory admitted to the hallowed halls of science, the theory had to be based upon well-accepted empirical laws, then indeed the major effort in the discipline had to be to go out and discover empirical laws. Since scholars were trying to find empirical regularities, the major focus for political scientists doing research was on questions of method—of how to operationalize variables adequately and of the proper kind of statistical test to use to assert relationships between variables. These are essential questions of an empirically based political science. But their dominance during the past several decades places the questions of how to describe political relationships in a quantitative manner above how to gain an adequate understanding of the processes involved in the relevant world of inquiry.

Further, the positivist perspective on the necessity of building political science anew, based on a rock bottom of quantitative empirical research, dominated the instruction given to graduate students in our discipline. Given the recruitment pattern into the discipline, entering students have frequently evinced shock when presented with this perspective on the nature of the discipline. High school students are rarely exposed to anything called political science until their junior or senior year. By that time most students have already taken mathematics, science, history, literature, and languages. Many students select a college major early from one of the subjects they took in high school and found interesting and challenging. Students who enjoy abstract thinking and mathematics may have already selected mathematics or a science that allows them to pursue these interests prior to any introduction to political science (see Lave and March, 1975).

The first introduction to political science qua high school civics does not attract the more theoretically and mathematically inclined students either. The focus on current events in high school civics courses associates political science with the study of current events for many students. This association is reinforced in college. At many universities large numbers of freshmen take an introduction to American government course where the emphasis is on the current structure and political behavior of American national government. Given the clientele and texts available, most of these courses are descriptive and include a heavy dose of current events.

Students who are interested in power struggles and learning the inside story related to current world crises are attracted. Students who are interested in more abstract intellectual endeavors are turned off. Majoring in political science does not alter the picture. Students can major in political science and never be introduced to political philosophy or the rigorous development of any type of modern political theory. Few of our undergraduates take more than minimal requirements in logic, philosophy, mathematics, or economics; and few take statistics as undergraduates.

Students entering graduate school with this type of background react to logical positivism in an extremely bimodal fashion. Some students vehemently reject the position. They either drop out of political science during their first year or simply develop a graduate program that does not require them to use theory rigorously or to learn quantitative methods. These students tend to ally themselves with faculty who are still fighting the antiquantitative war. Other students may have accepted the position too naively and wholeheartedly. If the position is accepted totally, what does this mean to a young colleague in political science?

The belief system includes the following propositions. For a discipline to be a science, it must have certain types of theories.

For a set of logically connected statements to be a theory, they must *start* with a well-known empirical law. For a statement to be considered an empirical law, quantitative data must be gathered and analyzed, and clear-cut and consistent patterns must repetitively be found. For students exposed to this position early in their careers, the import of their new scientific religion was that political science had *no* theory. David Easton (1953: 4), for example, asserted that:

> Clearly, if political science could arrive at . . . at general theory, the understanding of political life that it would give would be both profound and extensive. There is no need consequently to point out that such a theory would be desirable because of its utility. The only thing that is not apparent, however, is that the formulation of such a theory is a possible and necessary step along the road to reliable and perceptive knowledge about politics.

> No such theory is visible on the horizons of political research in the United States today.

For some political scientists, political science itself began in the 1950s. In a paper I read this past spring, for example, repeated references were made to the *classical* work in the field. All of the works cited were written after 1960!

With the "rock bottom" approach, as Popper (1965) calls it, scientific theories could not be constructed until political science had undertaken substantial hard-nosed empirical work to find the empirical laws to become the bedrock of the discipline. With missionary zeal, several generations of young colleagues went forth to collect data so that a political science could be constructed using their empirical findings as *the* foundation. Many of the early generations in this revolution were armed for the foray with minimal statistical training and no training in mathematics or logic. Changes slowly appeared in our journals. First, a few cross-tabulations were interspersed among what previously had been predominantly textual material. Correlation matrices appeared next. Multiple regression techniques were then introduced. More recently, a whole spectrum of advanced multivariate statistics has been displayed.

As methods have become more sophisticated, graduate students of more recent times faced even more perplexing problems. Those who did not reject the mainstream approach realized that they must acquire substantial methodological training just to read the major journals. Given that our recruitment pattern into the discipline has not fundamentally changed, most entering graduate students still have no philosophical, logical, mathematical, or statistical training as undergraduates. Consequently, in order to gain minimal levels of quantitative training, many graduate students take heavy courseloads in statistics and methods and fewer courses where they might be exposed to the development of systematic substantive theories.

The combined effect of this recruitment process interacting with this type of socialization may have produced a "know nothing" era in the discipline. Many scholars who presumed they were building our new empirical foundation did indeed know very little about substance and about the relationship of the statistical languages they used to the absence of theoretical models to which the language of data analysis should have been related. The criteria for what would be accepted as "facts" became a significant correlation coefficient or a high R^2, even when it meant the acceptance of nonsense or the rejection of long-established knowledge.

It is, of course, hard to characterize political science as being of one piece. Contained within the same discipline are so many individuals following such different approaches. However, during the past several decades a number of young political scientists considered themselves to be in the vanguard of the discipline. They saw themselves creating the empirical foundation for the final development of a science. They rejected the work of those who had gone before them. It is their work that largely dominated our major journals.

During the 1960s many political scientists accepted, for example, the frequently repeated statement that "political structure doesn't matter." As Dye (1966: 297) expressed it, "political variables do not count for much in shaping public policy." The fact that political variables accounted for a small proportion of the variance in government expenditure levels after economic and social variables had first been entered in multiple regression equations was taken as "proof" that institutional variables did not matter and should not be the subject of a mature science (see Dawson and Robinson, 1963; Hofferbert, 1966, 1972).[2]

The way a process is conceptualized should affect the analytical techniques to be used for estimating statistical parameters in empirical models of that process (Wright, 1976; Stonecash, 1978; Johnston, 1972; Hanushek and Jackson, 1977). Multiple regression techniques were first developed to examine the independent effect of land, labor, and fertilizer in agricultural productivity (see Ezekiel and Fox, 1959). Since each of these variables was conceptualized as *independent* and its effect on productivity was *additive,* the general linear model underlying multiple regression was the appropriate theoretical language for stating how these variables would be related to a dependent variable. I seriously doubt that one could find many statements in Hobbes, *The Federalist,* or Tocqueville that conceptualized the effect of institutions in a manner similar to that of fertilizer added to labor and land to produce corn (see V. Ostrom, 1980, 1982). In the last decade, as models of *how* political structure affects the pattern of relationships among economic, social, and technological variables have been formulated and tested, scholars have found important structural effects (see Carmines, 1974; Wright, 1976; Frey and Pommerehne, 1978; Summers and Wolfe, 1977; Phillips and Votey, 1972; E. Ostrom and Whitaker, 1973; Parks, 1979; Parks and E. Ostrom, 1981).

The languages of data analysis and method have dominated the languages of theory construction during much of the past two decades. As Sprague points out in Chapter 4, reliance on certain methods, because they are perceived to be more scientific, can coerce political scientists to ignore important theoretical questions. He is particularly concerned with the overreliance on *national* probability samples. Without adding contextual variables to individual records of a national sample, scholars can only examine how individuals, who have been plucked from their environments, acquire political attitudes. Important theoretical questions, relating political learning to context, cannot be pursued using most of the massive data sets already collected about the American electorate.

It is essential for empirical researchers to learn the languages of data analysis and to learn them early in their careers. Our undergraduate programs could all be strengthened by advising students of the importance of mathematics and statistics to an undergraduate major in political science. But a central task of the coming era is to reverse this domination so that the development of theory precedes the choice of appropriate methods to test a theory.

Fortunately, many scholars in the discipline, including the authors of chapters in this volume, are taking major steps to reestablish the priority of theory over data collection and analysis. Moreover, theory has also come to mean for many political scientists a set of logically connected statements without the requirement that assumptions used in a theory have themselves *already* been established as empirical laws. The covering-law perspective has not been replaced with another dominant philosophy of science. Among the important alternative views are those of Kuhn (1970), Lakatos (1971), and Habermas (1973). Among the authors who have provided useful overviews of the different traditions and important attempts at synthesis are Moon (1975), Toulmin (1977), and Shapiro (1981).

The essays in this volume reflect the subtle change occurring across political science and the sister disciplines of economics, sociology, and psychology. The first essay in this volume, by G. R. Boynton, is inspired by the work of Susanne Langer. Boynton argues that scientific advances have come when theorists have found principles by which they can order events that appear incommensurable and relate these events to one another. This places the focus for scientific advance on theoretical breakthroughs. The most important part of a theoretical breakthrough, according to Boynton, is an organizing principle. Terms are defined for the purpose of the relevant organizing principle. Proper names are no longer used. If events that were thought to be incommensurable are included within the same theoretical classification, it may also be the case that empirical references that share similar names may not be included in the same set when looked at from a theoretical perspective.

Boynton's chapter can be viewed as an inquiry into what is the "right type of law" for social scientists. The right type of law, he argues, is highly specific and relates a limited number of variables to each other under stated conditions. The conditions of a theory state the values of other variables that must be closely approximated for the posited theoretical relations to hold among explanatory variables. The "other" variables condition the type of relationships among the explanatory variables stated in the theory. By stressing the importance of stating the essential conditions for an organizing principle to operate, Boynton urges social scientists to try to understand the logic of relatively contained situations where the conditions structuring a situation are specified. His notion, therefore, of theory pertains to the organizing principles used to understand particular types of situations structured in specific ways (see also Barry, Chapter 5).

The importance of structuring conditions is central to the argument made by Roger Benjamin concerning the historical nature of social-scientific knowledge. Benjamin argues that the relationships found *within* political systems may vary across historical time periods. Different historical periods are for Benjamin what the concept of a laboratory is for Boynton. Within a laboratory the scientist structures an experiment to study dynamic change while carefully controlling other variables. Whenever the scientist changes the fundamental structure of the experiment, the scientist produces diachronic change in the laboratory.

As Boynton points out, the concept of a laboratory is a mental frame. Social scientists, studying the ongoing stream of events within real political systems, cannot set the parameters of variables that structure political processes. In times of relative political and social stability, the "experimental conditions" remain unchanged. However, in times of major societal development, the level of diachronic change may be so great as to make the study of dynamics futile until the consequence of change in structure can be examined.

Benjamin compares the prevalent theories used to explain political processes within industrial societies in the 1960s, with the theories used in the 1980s. He reasons that new theories will be needed to understand the macro- and microeconomic forces at work in postindustrial as contrasted with industrial systems. Four theories are currently evolving that Benjamin (Chapter 3) feels will be the source of our understanding of behavior in the remainder of the twentieth century. The four theories are (1) Mancur Olson's recent theory of stable societies and economic decline, (2) the product cycle theory, (3) the collective goods theory, and (4) critical theory. Benjamin concludes from his review of these diverse theories that "it is not business as usual in postindustrial societies." This leads him to argue that political scientists must understand the changing macro political-economic structure before they can explain regularity in micro behavior. Further, he argues the regularity in microrelationships in one historical period may be dramatically different in another.

John Sprague (Chapter 4) also examines the relationship between broader social structure and microanalysis. However, while Benjamin is interested in international political economies as they have an impact on political relationships within nation-states, Sprague is interested in the structure of neighborhood-level political attitudes as they may affect the determinants of individual political attitudes. Both ask how microrelationships can be examined within a macrostructure; however, the levels of their analyses differ dramatically.

The fundamental theoretical question that Sprague addresses is, "What are the mechanisms that connect microenvironments with individual political behavior? Or, more boldly put, how does social structure coerce individual behavior?" This is an interesting question for Sprague to address, because he has been interested for many years in macro processes. Sprague develops

an organizing principle to answer the puzzle of how the environment impinges upon relationships among individual political-
attitude variables. His organizing principle differs from the
model of the individual using the traditional assumptions of
neoclassical economics. Rather, he posits a model of information processing in the individual that structures the processes
through which individuals acquire political attitudes. His work
exemplifies a nonrational choice model that is based on a
foundation of methodological individualism.

While Boynton draws on the work of Susanne Langer for
inspiration about how to develop coherent theory in political
science, Brian Barry (Chapter 5) relies upon Mill. Mill, according
to Barry, stresses the problem that social scientists face given
the multiplicity of causes simultaneously affecting the processes
of interest. By isolating some relatively simple cases, in a process similar to the mental laboratory that Boynton posits, Mill
argues that one may be able to ascertain how some small
systems operate when isolated from the impact of other con-
founding variables. However, such findings about one micro-
system may not hold over time and place if structuring variables
change dramatically. While we may be able to establish empirical trends, " 'we cannot use them with any confidence as a
basis for prediction unless we have reason to expect the underlying conditions to remain unaltered' " (Mill, quoted by Barry,
Chapter 5). Benjamin's stress on the importance of history is
also consistent with Mill's analysis.

The cumulative effect of the chapters by Boynton, Benjamin,
and Barry should lead to a sense of humility on the part of
social scientists concerning what it is possible to do. All three
scholars argue that when conditions are well specified and
isolated, it is possible to develop rigorous theory for how some
variables interact with others. However, the number of variables
in the conditioning requirements may be large. Gaining a hold
on how all those variables interact, if major diachronic change
occurs, may be beyond our capabilities. Barry argues that this
may leave a limited role for the social scientist, but he also

argues that it would be "absurd to reject it in the pursuit of something more ambitious but actually useless."

The advantage of economics, according to Barry, has been its focus on a confined part of social life where institutions tightly structure the set of available options for participants and the range of effects. Given some simple behavioral laws about how individuals value outcomes, it is possible to develop relatively well-supported theory about the behavioral tendencies, given the nature of immediate situations. Barry then asks what kind of theory may enable social scientists to understand nonmarket processes. He turns to the work of Mancur Olson and shows how it has been applied by Popkin to a different setting with considerable fruitfulness. He also illustrates how Hardin has reexamined the underlying model of the individual to develop a more general theory than originally developed by Olson.

Barry further addresses the question of whether there is a necessary ideological content to an assumption of methodological individualism. Methodological individualism does not require any particular assumptions about individual motivation; rather, it simply insists that an adequate level of motivation be developed. Barry argues that there is nothing ideological about the methodological principle even though some applications are ideological. Sprague illustrates in his chapter a micro theory of motivation that is *not* an economic theory. Sprague demonstrates what Barry says can be done. Kiser and Ostrom also return to the same theme in the last chapter.

J. Donald Moon (Chapter 6) further explores the questions of how individuals make decisions and what types of theory enable scholars to advance understandings of political phenomena. Two fundamental strategies used by political scientists are identified by Moon: the interpretative approach, which he argues does not draw upon general laws and theories, and the theoretical approach, which does. Moon reexamines the situation facing European leaders in the 1930s and their decision concerning macroeconomic policies. In this case, macrostructural variables do not appear to account for the difference in policy decisions made by Sweden and Germany compared to Britain. Within systems that were relatively similar in structure, one set of leaders adopted a theoretical explanation for how the economic world operated that differed from the economic theory used by the other sets of actors.

Kiser and Ostrom (Chapter 7) present a metatheoretical framework for the analysis and synthesis of a large body of political-economy literature. The microinstitutional political-economy literature they examine explains individual actions and aggregated results occurring in decision situations affected by institutional rules, the nature of goods, and the type of community. Further, they present the key aspects of this approach as a series of component working parts. In any particular theory, a scholar in this tradition will make implicit or explicit assumptions about the specific attributes of each of the working parts. What distinguishes this approach from that used by macropolitical economists is the prominence of a model of the individual at the central core of any particular model. Kiser and Ostrom return to the theme developed earlier by Barry and Sprague, that many different models of the individual are consistent with the principle of methodological individualism.

In their framework, any model of the individual will include assumptions about the individual's level of information, the individual's valuation, and the individual's calculation process for selecting among alternative actions or strategies. Thus, the narrow rational choice model of the individual used in neoclassical economics and by some formal theorists of political behavior is characterized by assumptions that the individual possesses complete information, the individual values a single, externally measurable value (such as profits or the probability of being reelected), and the individual selects that strategy which maximizes this value. A model of the individual drawing on the work of Herbert Simon would instead posit an individual with limited information and bounded capacities for processing information, with multiple goals, and with a calculation process involving limited search for satisfactory outcomes. The type of model of the individual that Sprague presents is characterized by an individual with incomplete information, multiple goals (political goals plus a desire to please those with whom he or she interacts regularly), and a learning strategy based on rewards or punishments meted out for the political attitudes expressed.

The Kiser and Ostrom framework thus provides for comparing political and economic theories that use the individual as a basic unit of analysis. There is a whole family of such theories. At times the "family" resemblance is difficult to discern. Some of the debates among proponents of one or another model of the individual have also tended to mask the fundamental similarity in the broad structure of these theories. The broad framework presented in the last chapter should enable scholars using different theories of individual behavior more closely to identify where their similarities and differences are. If we are ever to develop more general theories related to the political and economic world, we must be able to step back from the advocacy of any particular theory to examine how specific assumptions combined together make a difference and produce different explanations. It is hoped that the framework presented in this chapter will enable readers outside and within the tradition to identify some fundamental similarities in the work described.

This introduction began with the speculation than an era was ending in political science. Personally, I feel this may have been a necessary but unpleasant era in the discipline's growth, somewhat like adolescence. The tendency to reject the work of our predecessors and adopt new languages and new technologies in an effort to start over is an important phase of a discipline gaining maturity. But real maturity comes when the worth of past efforts is recognized and new languages and technologies are integrated with the best work of former times. In these chapters one finds many references to and uses of the work of political philosophers, a recognition of the importance of history, an awareness of diverse philosophies of science, a basic concern with the central place of theory in the development of the discipline, the use of formal models, and a recognition of the importance of rigorous methods in data analysis. While pessimism about the discipline has permeated the literature of political science during the past few decades, we may be moving into a more optimistic era. As theory precedes empirical work, and empirical studies help to refine our theoretical understanding of the world, the hoped-for cumulation in that understanding may finally occur. However, if we take the warnings of Boynton, Barry, and Benjamin seriously, the cumulation we do achieve will be limited in scope to specific types of theoretically defined situations rather than sweeping theories of society as a whole.

NOTES

1. See also the excellent discussion of the covering-law model in Moon, 1975.
2. This tradition of work has been strongly criticized for its ad hoc nature by Jacob and Lipsky (1968), Fry and Winters (1970), Uslander and Weber (1975), Godwin and Shepard (1976), and Frey and Pommerehne (1978).

REFERENCES

Brodbeck, M. [ed.] (1968) *Readings in the Philosophy of the Social Sciences.* New York: Macmillan.
Carmines, E. G. (1974) "The mediating influence of state legislatures on the linkage between interparty competition and welfare policies." *American Political Science Review* 68: 1118-1124.
Dawson, R. E. and J. A. Robinson (1963) "Enter party competition, economic variables, and welfare policies in the American states." *Journal of Politics* 25 (May): 265-289.
Dye, T. R. (1966) *Politics, Economics, and the Public.* Chicago, IL: Rand McNally.
Easton, D. (1953) *The Political System.* New York: Knopf.
Ezekiel, M. and K. A. Fox (1959) *Methods of Correlation and Regression Analysis.* New York: John Wiley.
Falco, M. J. (1973) *Truth and Meaning in Political Science.* Columbus, OH: Merrill.
Feyerabend, P. K. (1970) "Against method: outline of an anarchistic theory of knowledge," pp. 17-130 in M. Radner and S. Winokur (eds.) *Minnesota Studies in the Philosophy of Science* (Vol. 4). Minneapolis: University of Minnesota Press.
Frey, B. S. and W. W. Pommerehne (1978) "Toward a more theoretical foundation for empirical policy analysis." *Comparative Political Studies* 11 (October): 311-336.
Fry, B. R. and R. R. Winters (1970) "The politics of redistribution." *American Political Science Review* 64 (June): 508-522.

Godwin, R. K. and W. B. Shepard (1976) "Political processes and public expenditures: a re-examination based on theories of representative government." *American Political Science Review* 70 (December): 1127-1135.

Goldberg, A. S. (1963) "Political science as science," pp. 26-36 in N. W. Polsby, R. A. Dentler, and P. A. Smith (eds.) *Politics and Social Life.* Boston: Houghton Mifflin.

Habermas, J. (1973) *Theory and Practice.* Boston: Beacon Press.

Hanushek, E. A. and J. E. Jackson (1977) *Statistical Methods for Social Scientists.* New York: Academic Press.

Hempel, C. G. (1965) *Aspects of Scientific Explanation.* New York: Free Press.

Hofferbert, R. I. (1966) "The relation between public policy and some structural and economic variables in the American states." *American Political Science Review* 60 (March): 63-82.

——— (1972) "State and community policy studies: a review of comparative input-output analyses," pp. 3-72 in J. A. Robinson (ed.) *Political Science Annual* (Vol. 3). Indianapolis: Bobbs-Merrill.

Jacob, H. and M. Lipsky (1968) "Outputs, structure, and power: an assessment of changes in the study of state and local government." *Journal of Politics* 30: 510-538.

Johnston, J. (1963) *Econometric Methods.* New York: McGraw-Hill.

Kuhn, T. F. (1970) *The Structure of Scientific Revolutions* (2nd ed.). Chicago: University of Chicago Press.

Lakatos, I. (1971) "History of science and its rational reconstructions," pp. 91-136 in R. F. Cohen and M. W. Wartofsky (eds.) *Boston Studies in the Philosophy of Science* (Vol. 8). New York: Humanities Press.

Laslett, P., W. G. Runciman, and Q. Skinner (1972) *Philosophy, Politics, and Society* (fourth series). Oxford: Blackwell.

Lave, C. A. and J. G. March (1975) *An Introduction to Models in the Social Sciences.* New York: Harper & Row.

MacIntyre, A. (1967) "The idea of a social science." *Proceedings of the Aristotelian Society* suppl. 41: 112-130.

Moe, T. (1979) "On the scientific status of rational models." *American Journal of Political Science* 23 (February): 215-243.

Moon, J. D. (1975) "The logic of political inquiry," pp. 131-228 in F. I. Greenstein and N. Polsby (eds.) *Political Science: Scope and Theory* (Vol. 1). Reading, MA: Addison-Wesley.

Nagel, E. (1961) *The Structure of Science: Problems in the Logic of Scientific Explanation.* New York: Harcourt Brace Jovanovich.

Ostrom, E. and G. P. Whitaker (1973) "Does local community control of police make a difference? some preliminary findings." *American Journal of Political Science* 19 (February): 48-76.

Ostrom, V. (1980) *Leviathan and Democracy.* Bloomington: Indiana University, Workshop in Political Theory and Policy Analysis.

——— (forthcoming) *The Political Theory of a Compound Republic* (rev. ed.). New Brunswick, NJ: Transaction.

Parks, R. B. (1979) "Assessing the influence of organization on performance: a study of police services in residential neighborhoods." Bloomington: Indiana University, Workshop in Political Theory and Policy Analysis.

――― and E. Ostrom (1981) "Developing and testing complex models of urban service systems," pp. 171-200 in T. N. Clark (ed.) *Urban Policy Analysis: Directions for Future Research* (Vol. 21). Beverly Hills, CA: Sage Publications.

Phillips, L. and H. L. Votey, Jr. (1972) "An economic analysis of the current effects of law enforcement on criminal activity." *Journal of Criminal Law, Criminology and Police Science* 63 (September): 330-342.

Popper, K. R. (1965) *The Logic of Scientific Discovery.* New York: Harper & Row.

Przeworski, A. and H. Teune (1970) *The Logic of Comparative Social Inquiry.* New York: John Wiley.

Rudner, R. S. (1966) *Philosophy of Social Science.* Englewood Cliffs, NJ: Prentice-Hall.

Shapiro, M. J. (1981) *Language and Political Understanding: The Politics of Discursive Practices.* New Haven, CT: Yale University Press.

Stonecash, J. (1978) "Local policy analysis and autonomy: on intergovernmental relations and theory specification." *Comparative Urban Research* 5, 2/3: 5-23.

Summers, A. A. and B. L. Wolfe (1977) "Do schools make a difference?" *American Economic Review* 67 (September): 639-652.

Toulmin, S. E. (1977) "From form to function: philosophy and history of science in 1950s and now." *Daedalus* 106, 3: 143-162.

Uslander, E. M. and R. E. Weber (1975) "The 'single politics' of redistribution: toward a model of the policy-making process in the American states." *American Politics Quarterly* 3 (April): 130-170.

Winch, P. (1958) *The Idea of a Social Science.* London: Rutledge & Kegan Paul.

Wright, G. C., Jr. (1976) "Linear models for evaluating conditional relationships." *American Journal of Political Science* 20 (May): 349-373.

2

On Getting from Here to There

Reflections on Two Paragraphs and Other Things

G. R. BOYNTON

These assumptions are satisfied to various degrees by the applications mentioned earlier. Swirling, turbid effects are bound to occur in any large diameter pipe. This limits the usefulness of our law in studying water pipes, oil pipelines, grain chutes, etc. Blood vessels flex: their dimensions change a little. Blood surges because of the heart's pumping action; thus the flow is not steady-state. Oxygen and nutrients leave a blood vessel by osmosis through the pipe's wall and wastes are added to the blood flow, so that fluid is only approximately conserved.

Despite these and other practical short-comings, Poiseuille's Law is a valid simplification of viscous fluid flow. *It is the right sort of law:* $v(r)$ is zero at the pipe wall and increases steadily as r decreases and we approach the pipe's center. It has a solid, well-understood theoretical basis. We can really calculate with it, as we shall shortly see. And in the laboratory, the assumed conditions can be made almost true, giving a practical way to measure the viscosity coefficient k for

AUTHOR'S NOTE: Support for this research was granted by the National Science Foundation, Grant SPI 78-19060. The Center for International Policy Studies is supported by Grant 750-0514 from the Ford Foundation.

any fluid. This coefficient is a fundamental property of the fluid,
important in design and engineering work [Tuchinsky, 1978: 5].

I do not believe that anyone would want to assert that
political science is one of the advanced sciences. Some might
even assert that it is an act of faith to think of political science
as being on the uphill side of becoming a science—asserting
instead that we are still searching for the slope. But we have
made some progress in the last thirty years. We have learned
something about doing empirical research, and in the process we
have developed a considerable panoply of tools for conducting
research effectively. That is a necessary, if not a sufficient,
condition for making the trip up the hill.

The most glaring weakness in our progress has been the
discontinuity between theory and research. It is not that we do
not have both in profusion. We could fill our publication outlets
many times over with research reports and theorizing. But
theory does not seem to lead naturally and directly to research,
and research does not seem either to be grounded in or to lead
to theory. They go their separate ways. Having been a member
of the "research camp," I have puzzled over this conundrum for
more than a decade. I am still puzzled.

It seems clear that we do not understand the relationship
between theory and "the world" the theory is about. The event
that precipitated this collection of ideas was reading the two
paragraphs that are quoted above. It exemplifies an understanding of that relationship, which is, I think, quite foreign to our
thinking about the matter. But this was only the precipitating
event. Now that I have spent some time studying logic and set
theory, there are a lot of thoughts circulating in my head that
need some expression.

This is a collection of ideas on the way to arguments. It is not
one integrated argument, although the sections revolve around a
limited number of themes. But everything revolves around one
question. How would I recognize a theory if I stumbled over
one? My interest is in theorizing. I want to understand what one
would have to do to produce a theory. Thus it is not so much
the finished product that is the subject of these sections as it is
what I can learn about the process of getting to the finished

product from thinking about aspects of the finished product that is my subject. Thus the title, "On Getting from Here to There." I do not think we are there. That is, I am not satisfied with the theories we have produced, and I want to explore how I might go about getting to a finished product that I like.

There is a mutilated aphorism that aptly expresses the spirit in which this chapter is written:

Now I see through a glass darkly.
Maybe tomorrow—face to face.

THE RIGHT SORT OF LAW

Viscosity is not my favorite subject; I had never given much thought to how fluids manage to get through pipes, and I do not expect to devote much more attention to the problem in the future. What I found intriguing in reading about Poiseuille's Law was the assertion that it is the right sort of law. What does it mean to say that something is the right sort of law? That question cannot be answered without some description of the law and the reasons that the author felt the need to make the assertion. That is what this section is designed to give. The most rapid way to get through the description is to quote a couple of paragraphs.

When a thick, sticky (viscous) fluid flows through a pipe, it does not all flow at the same speed. Instead the fluid closest to the wall of the pipe suffers so much friction with the wall that it hardly moves at all, while fluid closer to the central axis of the pipe moves more rapidly. The fluid's speed increases steadily as the distance from the wall increases. Because of circular symmetry, the effect is that of concentric tubes of fluid sliding over one another. We call this laminar flow: each lamina or layer of fluid moves at its own speed. Different laminae move at different speeds [Tuchinsky, 1978: 1].

The peculiar pattern of flow of viscous liquids through pipes and other types of containers is the problem. Poiseuille, who was studying the flow of blood through blood vessels, found that the velocity of the particles of fluid at a distance r centimeters out from the center axis of the pipe is

$$v(r) = \frac{P}{4kL} (R^2 - r^2) \qquad \text{(cm/sec.)}$$

where v is velocity of a particle; r is distance in centimeters out from the center axis of the pipe; R is radius of the pipe in centimeters (thus, $0 \leqslant r \leqslant R$); L is length of the pipe; P is pressure change down the length of the pipe; and k is coefficient of viscosity. It turns out that this law is true for any liquid subject to the following assumptions (Tuchinsky, 1978: 2):

(1) There must be no turbidity in the fluid. This means that there is no swirling; particles of fluid move in straight lines down the pipe.
(2) The speed of flow v is assumed to depend on r only. Thus v does not change as fluid moves down the length of the pipe, and it does not change with time; the flow is neither speeding up nor slowing down; it is steady state.
(3) The fluid is incompressable, that is, made up of particles that cannot be crushed or packed in closer together (by the forces present).
(4) Fluid is conserved, that is, neither created nor lost, in the pipe. Thus no fluid is leaking out through the pipe wall and no feeder-pipes are pouring fluid in or out.
(5) The tube is horizontal and the (very slight) downward pulling effects of gravity are ignored.
(6) The pipe is a right-circular cylinder with constant dimensions L and R.
(7) There is so much friction at the wall that fluid there does not move at all. (Notice that $r = R$ leads to $v[r] = 0$.)
(8) One assumption that is not present: in other classes you may study so-called ideal fluids, in which particles slip frictionlessly by each other. We are assuming that each layer exerts a drag on the layer next-further-in. Ours is not an ideal fluid.

With these few assumptions the law holds.

One senses a certain defensiveness in the assertion: "Despite these and other practical short-comings . . . it is the right sort of law." If there were no problem in convincing others that this is the right sort of law then there would be no need for the assertion. So, why the assertion? The statement that this is the right sort of law follows the longish list of assumptions that must hold for the law to "work." It might be the number of assumptions necessary that precipitates the assertion. But I do not think that is the problem. Again, notice what is said in the paragraph that opened this chapter:

> These assumptions are satisfied to various degrees by the applica-
> tions mentioned earlier. Swirling, turbid effects are bound to occur
> in any large diameter pipe. This limits the usefulness of our law in
> studying water pipes, oil pipelines, grain chutes, etc. Blood vessels
> flex: their dimensions change a little. Blood surges because of the
> heart's pumping action; thus the flow is not steady-state. Oxygen
> and nutrients leave a blood vessel by osmosis through the pipe's wall
> and wastes are added to the blood flow, so that fluid is only
> approximately conserved [Tuchinsky, 1978: 5].

The problem would seem to be that the assumptions are only infrequently met in the world in which we live. The law is not about an ideal liquid, but it does seem to require ideal conditions (the laboratory) to work as stated. The practical utility of the law, at least as stated here, seems to be the problem. It does not fit the "real world" very well.

If the law does not apply in many practical situations in what sense can it be said to be the right sort of law?

> Despite these and other practical short-comings, Poiseuille's Law is a
> valid simplification of viscous fluid flow. It is the right sort of law:
> $v(r)$ is zero at the pipe wall and increases steadily as r decreases and
> we approach the pipe's center. It has a solid, well-understood theo-
> retical basis. We can really calculate with it, as we shall shortly see.
> And in the laboratory, the assumed conditions can be made almost
> true, giving a practical way to measure the viscosity coefficient k for
> any fluid. This coefficient is a fundamental property of the fluid,
> important in design and engineering work [Tuchinsky, 1978: 5].

The first thing to note is that it is characterized as a "valid simplification." It is not a description; it is a simplification. It is valid because the equation, which is the statement of the law, has the properties that are thought to characterize fluids: "v(r) is zero at the pipe wall and increases steadily as r decreases and we approach the pipe's center." It is also valid because it has a solid theoretical basis, which means that it can be deduced from a theory that is widely accepted. For any reader who would like to follow up on this assertion, I quote:

> If you know multivariable calculus and a little mathematical physics, you can read a clear derivation of Poiseuille's Law from basic ideas in elasticity and fluid flows [Slater and Frank, 1933].

In addition, the law has a very practical application. Under laboratory conditions it is possible to assign a number to each liquid, its viscosity coefficient, which is an important property of each liquid and which can be used in planning (engineering). So, it is the right sort of law.

Thus endeth the story of Poiseuille's Law.

WHY PRINCIPLES?

A small incident occurred about one week before I came across the description of Poiseuille's Law. I was walking across campus at shortly after noon, and I encountered the shrill blast of a whistle being used by a construction company. Somewhere there is someone who could explain to me why my ears were nearly pierced. I am sure that there is someone who can explain to me how sound waves are propagated through the air, and I am sure that there is someone who can explain the relationship between sound waves and the pain I experienced at having to listen to the whistle. Based on their theories, we could set up a nice little experiment that would predict my level of pain, depending on how the whistle (or on which whistle) was blown.

But while I was walking along, listening to the whistle, a large truck passed between the whistle and me. There were a few seconds of relief. Along with the relief I realized that if we had been conducting an experiment, "relief" would have consti- tuted a very peculiar measurement. The whistle blew just the same as always. But my ears did not feel the same amount of pain. Shall I accuse their theories of being faulty?

Most of the world is irrelevant to a good theory. Put another way, most of the world is exogenous to a theory. But in the real world, everything is connected to everything else. So how do the two scientists who are explaining my earache defend their theories against the charge that the theories are faulty when they did not predict what actually happened? Scientist A says, "I have a theory about the propagation of sound waves. I can take into account with this theory what will happen in the case of obstacles, but it is not my business to predict obstacles. The incidence of obstacles is irrelevant to my theory." Scientist B says, "I only deal (theoretically) with sound waves and human experience of sound waves. How the sound waves got to be what they are at any given moment is irrelevant to my theory."

There are now two theories. Both are viewed as excellent. But if they had made a prediction it would have turned out to be false. Why, then, do we call them good theories? We call them good theories because when we want to we can arrange things so that there are no obstructions and their predictions hold; we call this the laboratory setting. In addition, one builds a concert hall so as to minimize (among other things) obstructions to sound waves. The predictions work. Whenever the quality of sound is important to us we take special pains to make sure that obstructions will not occur. Obstructions are not irrelevant to the theories, but the incidence of obstructions is. We do not ask the physicist to predict the incidence of trucks. That is a job that is too difficult so we leave it to social scientists.

A principle is useful if you can show that it works and the limits under which it will work. One is not asked to predict when the limits will be exceeded. At least that is the way we treat physical principles.

We do so because we can often arrange the world so that the limits are only rarely exceeded. At least we think we can, and if we cannot, we do not blame that on the physicist.

Assume that a social scientist might come up with a principle. This social scientist would be required to tell us not only what the principle is but also the limits beyond which that principle will not produce the "main" predictions. Can we imagine arranging the world so that the limits are only rarely exceeded?

Would we be willing, even, to accept the notion that there are limits beyond which the principle will not work? Arranging the social world so that the limits are rarely exceeded is much more difficult than building an auditorium. And we are rarely willing to concede that limits on social principles are not indications of failures in social principles; witness the current standing of the Phillip's curve.

Why, then, should a social scientist try to find/develop/articulate/propagate principles? Because there is nothing else. The only alternative is explaining literally everything at the same time. And that is as impossible for the social scientist as it is for the physicist.

OUR S.O.P. TO SCIENCE

In this section I want to draw the moral from the first two sections as clearly and explicitly as possible. First, I want to indicate what I am rejecting, based on the reflections in the first two sections. Then I will turn to a somewhat more positive reconstruction.

What if a "typical" political scientist wanted to study viscosity? How would this "typical" political scientist proceed?[1] The first step would be to take a sample of all possible vessels through which liquids are known to flow. They would be big and little, straight and crooked, interconnected and not interconnected. One has only to imagine a sample of the pipes one knows about to have some idea about what this collection of vessels would look like. Next one would collect a sample of liquids. Then one would get a machine that would push the various liquids through the pipes at different pressure levels. The next step would be to run the liquids through the pipes at different levels of pressure and collect information on flow out of the pipes over time. Once this data had been gathered, it would be plugged into the general linear model, and summary results would flow from one's local computer.

The results that would be obtained from the analysis described above could not be Poiseuille's Law. One cannot get to Poiseuille's Law by following the procedure outlined above, for two reasons. First, Poiseuille's Law is about the velocity of a single concentric circle of liquid. In order to get from the law to total flow, it is necessary to integrate across the laminae making up the liquid; the integration is based on the diameter of the pipe. The point is that Poiseuille's Law begins with a conception of flow of liquids that is quite different than that implied in the experimental design described above. It is that conception of liquid flow which makes it possible to arrive at the law. The second reason that one would not get Poiseuille's Law is that many of the assumptions that must hold for Poiseuille's Law to be an accurate description of liquid flow would have been violated in the experimental design I suggested. The measurements from the large pipes would contain "error" due to swirling effects. At least some of the pipes would be interconnected. There was no stipulation of a steady-state flow in the experimental design. Thus, there would be change in velocity of the liquid with time. I am not sure what one would get from the experimental design outlined above, but it could not be Poiseuille's Law.

The point I want to make is about the connection between ideas or theory or principles and description. Science is the connection of ideas and description. If one observes the *Standard Operating Procedure* of much of empirical political science, one is led to the conclusion that the link we expect to find between ideas or theory and description is that of empirical generalization. We expect to be able to develop our theory by looking at empirically general propositions. And we expect our theoretical formulations to predict general trends in empirical phenomena. This cannot be a wholly misguided conception of what science is about. Scientific theories are general and they are accurate descriptions. However, the connection between theory and description is rarely (never, if one adopts certain views in the philosophy of science) the brute-force empirical generalization described above. The connection between theory and description is normally a good deal more complicated than empirical generalization.

The next several sections explicate ways in which this connection can be made effectively. But at least two of the points are already implicit in these first three sections, and they can be noted here. First, the ideas of a science prescribe how to look at empirical phenomena. The empirical world is just what it is. One might speak of either divining or imposing on the stuff of experience the order we seek. We seek an order to experience, and that order is to be found in a theory that says, "Look at the phenomenon in this way; when you do you will see the order that has been eluding you." Second, the order is most clearly seen in very special circumstances. In laboratory sciences the important function of laboratories is to make explicit what those special circumstances are. Poiseuille's Law is an accurate description only when a number of conditions have been met. When those conditions are not met, the order that is there is much more difficult to observe. This trick is more difficult in nonlaboratory science, but it is possible if we know what we are looking for and explicitly set out to accomplish it.

Both describing and theorizing are necessary to science, and there is no necessary order in which the two must proceed. At times description has come first and theorizing has followed, as scientists tried to make comprehensible empirical phenomena that seemed inexplicable. At other times theory has preceded description. A very good idea suggested research that justified the idea. But the argument of these first three sections is that the connection between the two is somewhat more complex than political scientists have often believed.

FROM PARTICULARS TO PRINCIPLES

The world presents itself as a never-ending string of particular occurrences. Despite the particularity of our experience, we are quite certain that there is order underlying these occurrences. If there were no order, every event would be unrelated to every other event. Learning, anticipation, and planning would be impossible. More generally, survival as we know it would be impossible. We do survive, as we know survival, and thus there is order. The role of systematic inquiry is to lay bare the order that we can find in the particularity of the world as we experience it. The order of the natural world has proved to be more tractable to the human imagination than has the order of the social world. There is so great a gap between the systematicity of our knowledge of the physical and social world that many have asserted that social science is very unlikely to be possible. But we have survived, so far, in a decidedly social world; thus there must be order. The challenge to our imagination is to explicate the order that inheres in social relations.

The first three sections had a specific objective. That objective was to assert that the relationship between laws or principles and the particularity in which we experience the world was not a simple matter of description. If the relationship is something other than describing particularity, then I must now try to say something about what it is. This will be the task of the next several sections. In a sense I will be trying to answer the question, How does one get from particularities to principles? But if this is taken as a question of history, I am doomed, for there are probably as many different ways as there are individuals who have made this trip. Instead the answer must be couched in some other terms. So I will try to answer the question, What is a principle that it may explicate order among particulars?

I will begin by quoting two brief passages from Susanne Langer, which present in summary form the two points that will be elaborated in this section:

> Whenever we may truly claim to have a science, we have found some principle by which different things are related to each other as just so many forms of one substrata, or material, and everything that can be treated as a new variation belongs to that science [Langer, 1953: 23].

> Often it is hard to believe that a philosopher or a scientist has any chance whatever of reducing widely different things to the same category, because they look and "feel" so incommensurable, but he has found a principle by which he can describe them as two forms of one substance, and we are amazed to see how precisely and usefully he then relates them [Langer, 1953: 26].

What is a principle that it may explicate order among particulars? It is that by which apparently incommensurable things are "related to each other as just so many forms of one substrata." There are two important aspects to any principle. The first is reduction of heterogeneity by defining "superficially" quite different things as being of one material or substance. The second aspect of the principle is the recognition of form or structure in this now homogenous substrata. The two are interwoven in the principle. Neither by itself is of much value along the road to building theory.

In a sense one may say that the first aspect of principles is nothing more than defining a set. The apparent incommensurability of the elements of the set is a before-the-fact phenomenon. Before a given set was defined no one may have thought about putting its particular elements together. But after the definition has been accepted by a discipline, there is no longer apparent incommensurability. The definition of the set or the putting together of these particular elements is taken for granted. But defining a set is very easy. Almost any elementary math textbook will tell you how it is done, that is, a recipe is presented for defining a set. If that was all there is to it, then our problems would have been over long ago. The real trick is the intuition that defining these particular elements or occurrences as a set will lead one to a very general, ordered set of relationships. This must, of course, be followed up by showing that the definition does lead to the anticipated order among particulars.

The second aspect of a principle is form or structure. One must initially have an intuition of a form or structure that operates over the set of elements that has been defined. This is surely why formal languages have been so important in science, for formal languages are exclusively languages of structure. The original intuition must, of course, be tested and elaborated, but that is the subject of a later section. Some hunch about the structure operating over the defined set is necessary. For example, Poiseuille's original insight was the idea that liquids could be conceived as concentric rings that exert a drag on the next layer or concentric ring out from the center of the pipe. Without this basic insight we would never have had Poiseuille's Law.

This definition of how a principle orders particulars is very general. I would now like to present an illustration. It is not confirmed science. It is an intuition in the making, but I hope it illustrates this definition in a political context. The testing and elaboration remains for the future.

The illustration begins by quoting three brief accounts of actions taken by government.

Hershey Bars' Price Increase
Not a Violation

The government said yesterday that a controversial nickel price hike for Hershey chocolate bars does not violate President Carter's voluntary price guidelines.

The Hershey increase was one of the first announced after President Carter made known the details of his anti-inflation plan Oct. 24, and became a matter of concern at a Carter press conference the week before last.

The overall price increase for all products made by the Hershey Chocolate Co., of Hershey, Pa., works out to 8.9 percent. During 1976 and 1977, the base period for Carter's anti-inflation program, Hershey's price increases averaged 13.75 percent [Washington Post, 1978c].

Family-Planning Bull Helps
Lower Birth Rate

A very important factor in the Thai economic picture is an intelligent approach to birth control that World Bank mission head Hendrik van der Heiden says "appeals to the Thai sense of the funny and the frugal."

The Thais shun a direct monetary payment for the farmer who gets a vasectomy (as was the case in the disastrous, involuntary program tried by former prime minister Gandhi in India). Instead, the cows of the Thai farmer who has had a vasectomy get the lifetime services of what is amusingly called "the family-planned bull."

This has worked so well that Thailand may be the one country where vasectomies are constrained not by demand but by the supply of money available for the government subsidy to the doctors. There are some good-natured titters—but that's all—when the "family-planning bull" shows up.

Coupled with other forms of birth control, including the controversial Depo-Provera injection, which has been used here for years, the population growth rate has dropped from 3.2 percent annually in the 1960's to 2.5 percent and the Thais think it reasonable to predict that is will dip to 1.8 percent in 1985 [Washington Post, 1978b].

Tougher Fire Rules
Sought on Furniture

Citing an estimated 500 deaths caused by fires from cigarettes igniting furniture, the staff of a federal agency yesterday called for tough flammability standards for the upholstery industry.

The staff of the Consumer Product Safety Commission estimated that meeting the proposed fire standards would increase the price of a chair by $3.50 to $5.30 and the price of a sofa by $6.60 to $10.00.

The estimated total cost to the industry annually is between $57 million and $87 million, while the total increased cost to consumers will be $114 million to $174 million.

The staff pointed out, however, that economic losses from fires involving upholstered residential furniture total an estimated $540 million annually from death, injury and property damage.

The CPSC still must consider the staff proposal, which will be presented on Dec. 6, in a public session. On Dec. 20, industry will make its presentation. No date for a commission vote has been set. The proposed rule would not take effect for at least a year after final approval [Washington Post, 1978c].

I was recently invited to become a member of the Policy Studies Organization—along with, I presume, all other members of the American Political Science Association. One of the key elements in membership is receipt of their extensive set of publications. In reflecting on that publication program and these three newspaper stories I conclude two things. First, in a sense that organization would have no difficulty in making all three of the occurrences summarized in the newspaper stories commensurable; they are all instances of public policy, that is, they are all acts of government. However, incommensurability almost immediately appears in the publications for they are organized in terms of health policy, civil rights policy, defense policy, and so on. The defining characteristic of the "universal" set is that they are acts of government. This universal set is then differentiated in terms of a subject-matter classification of the aims of the policy. Second, I conclude that this definition provides very little in the way of a suggestion of structure or form operating over the set. The only structure implicit in this definition is that government is doing something about something.

I want to give an alternative way of making the incommensurables commensurable. This will be done through a definition of governing or a definition of elements that would fall into the set labeled acts of governing.

"Governing is reducing variety in behavior." This is, of course, not my own definition; it is taken from the work of Ross Ashby, whose interest was in governing of a considerably broader character than what "governments" do. The rather casual phrasing of this definition does not make very clear what is explicit in the definition when presented in formal language. Let me specify at least some of what is involved in the definition. How should one understand "variety in behavior" as it is used in this definition?

"Variety in behavior" refers to all of the possible actions that might be taken. For example, furniture manufacturers have a wide variety of materials that they might use in upholstering furniture. The furniture manufacturers "rule out" many of these materials. Few pieces of furniture are sold covered with tissue paper or leaves. But tissue paper and leaves are elements of the set of potential materials for covering furniture and thus part of the behavioral potential of furniture manufacturers. The Thai farmer may be acting in a way that will lead to increasing the size of his family or not. The Hershey Chocolate Company, and more generally all business enterprises in the United States, are engaged in the behavior of affixing prices to their products. Here is an example of a set of behavioral possibilities that is, in principle, infinite. The price could be any real number, and the set of real numbers is not bounded. Governing is the operation by which this very large behavioral potential is reduced or constrained to some subset. The physical manifestation of acts of governing are very diverse. In the Thai case it involves doctors and bulls. In the case of inflation in the United States in 1978-1979 it involves a program announced by the President and an office that oversees this voluntary program. One of the jobs of this office is to assure the world that the Hershey Company really is in compliance with the President's program; Hershey corporate leaders do not want to be labeled "bad guys." And the Consumer Product Safety Commission may promulgate a rule that could carry penalty of prosecution if it is not followed. But this definition identifies each of these, and many other actions as well, as operations that reduce potential variety in behavior to a particular subset.

I want to discuss one further example because it is so simple that both the potential variety in behavior and the governing of that potential variety are very easy to see. It is a political, though not a public policy, example.

> Two House Democrats reelected by landslide margins earlier this month received puzzling letters from President Carter's chief congressional liaison, who expressed regrets over the "results of the election."
>
> Rep. John Conyers, Jr. (D-Mich.), who won with 93 percent of the vote, and Rep. Peter H. Kostmayer (D-Pa.), who won with 63 percent, received the letters from the office of Frank Moore.
>
> "Knowing of your long and difficult campaign, I was truly sorry that the results of Tuesday's election," the letter read.
>
> "I enjoyed working with you in the last Congress, and I will miss your contribution to the legislative process . . . You can be proud of your record of accomplishment. I wish you every success in the future" [Washington Post, 1978d].

It is not difficult to figure out the potential variety of behavior in this situation. There were two letters and two classes of candidates. There was a letter of congratulations; let this be represented by C. There was a letter of condolences; let this be represented by C'. The candidates were divided into winners (W) and losers (L). The potential variety in behavior is four;

these are the four combinations listed in the two lefthand columns below.

Canditates	Letter	Send Letter
W	C	Yes
W	C′	No
L	C	No
L	C′	Yes

In this case, governing begins with a rule that is listed in the righthand column above. But it also includes a list of the candidates and information about the class into which each of the candidates falls. And governing involves the assumption that the person who is to follow the rule is motivated to do so and can do it effectively. Thus, governing involves a rule, information, and the willingness and effectiveness of the person who is to use the information to follow the rule. If all of this works, then all candidates will receive the correct letter, and variety of behavior will have been reduced in the appropriate way, that is, it will have been reduced to a particular subset of the potential. But governing can break down at any one of the aspects of governing listed. We do not know where it broke down in Mr. Moore's communication with congressional candidates, but we would know where to look.

The advantage of this simple example is that it makes it possible to specify the general properties of governing in a context that is so simple that it is, in this case, obvious. But all of the general properties of governing are there. There is the potential variety that is to be reduced, and the mechanisms by which the variety reduction is to take place (rule, information, and willingness and effectiveness of the operational mechanism) are there also.

Let me now return to the question set for this section. What is a principle that it may order particulars? A principle orders particulars first by suggesting that one look at the particulars in a quite specific way. Look at all of these things in this way. Notice or attend to this aspect of the particulars. In the illustration given above one is admonished to look at apparently disparate activities as ways in which potential variety in behavior is reduced. At first that will seem a peculiar way of looking at health policy or defense policy. A part of attending to one aspect of particulars is that other aspects are ignored. Thus, some or even much of what one ordinarily attends to in looking at health policy may be "lost" in looking at it in this way. The advantage of doing this is that it makes incommensurables commensurable. Now all of the particulars are ordered by being instances of or examples of a specific type of phenomenon. Second, particulars are ordered through the suggestion that there is a specific structure operating over all of the particulars. In the example, that structure involves rules, information, and willingness and effectiveness of the mechanism that is regulating the variety in behavior. Thus, principles order particulars by making them all instances of a single class of phenomenon and by showing that there is one structure that operates over the entire class, that is, operates on each particular element of the set.

At this point I need to unscramble a potential ambiguity in the use of "principle" in the several sections of this chapter. I would like to do this by distinguishing between an organizing principle and a principle. When Susanne Langer wrote, "Whenever we may truly claim to have a science, we have found some principle by which different things are related to each other as just so many forms of one substrata," I believe she had an organizing principle in mind. When I paraphrased Ross Ashby, "Governing is reducing variety in behavior," I took this to be an organizing principle. This paraphrased statement is a shorthand way of referring to a number of propositions that do the two things Susanne Langer suggested a principle does. There are statements that define the set, and there are statements that make explicit the structure operating over the set. All of these statements are part of the organizing principle. Thus, an *organizing principle* is not a single proposition; it is a collection of propositions that serves as the starting point of a theory. A *principle,* on the other hand, is a single proposition. It may be one of the propositions of the organizing principle or it may be a proposition that can be deduced from the organizing principle. One of the principles that can be deduced from Ashby's

definition of governing is, "Governing is bounded by information." This is a single proposition based on or deduced from the
set of statements that define governing. In a comparable way,
Poiseuille's Law is a principle. It is a single proposition that can
be deduced from a more general collection of propositions (or
an organizing principle). Both of these principles have very
broad applications; Ashby's principle about information and
governing applies to a very general class of events, and Poiseuille's Law applies to all liquids. However, each is a single
proposition rather than what Susanne Langer had in mind as an
organizing principle. From this point on I will use the two
different expressions in order to avoid ambiguity.

In order to bring all of this to bear on ordinary political
science, I want to examine briefly two definitions used by
political scientists to show how they fall short of being either
organizing principles or principles.

Is there an organizing principle lurking in the writing on
"support"? I spent a lot of time thinking about support, and I
even did a good deal of empirical research using that concept.
But I was always bothered because something seemed to be
missing. Perhaps I can specify what I found missing by contrasting it with this definition of organizing principle. Support was
defined as a relationship between individual citizens and their
political communities, regimes, and political authorities. Then
support was classified into overt and covert support, diffuse and
specific support, and so forth.

Most of the research that has been done on support has
attempted to specify conditions under which individual citizens
will be supportive or not supportive. The problem is that the
relationship between the individual citizen and the community,
regime, and political authorities was never clearly specified.
Usually support was defined in terms of synonyms such as
"likes," "favors," "is positive toward."

This failure to specify structural properties of the relationship had two unfortunate consequences. First, there was a great
deal of argument about what was the most appropriate measurement of support. Was trust in government a measure of support
or was it something else? What about efficacy? And so on.
Second, support was thought to be important because in some

way it was related to the stability of the political community, political regime, and political authorities.

During the late 1960s and through the 1970s there has been a good deal of cynicism or lack of trust or negative feeling toward government among the citizens of the United States. Does that mean that the community, regime, and authorities were unstable? There has been a good deal of agitation during this period. But should that be viewed as support for changing the policy of government or lack of support for the community, regime, or authorities? We do not know how to answer that question because the definition of support does not tell us. There was a lot of cynicism about government, but the turnover of members of Congress declined. Is that an indication of stability or instability of authorities?

The definition of support does not specify the structure of the relationship between citizens and community, regime, and authorities. Thus, we can neither decide measurement questions (specify what is in and out of the set) nor decide whether the information we do have is consistent with that relationship. Without specifying the structure of the relationship, the reduction of incommensurables to commensurables is ambiguous, and we have no idea about the common structure operating over this set.

What is wrong with "recruitment"? I have also worked on recruitment a little. One possible definition of recruitment is that it is the process of obtaining and maintaining office. The phrase "obtaining and maintaining office" is quite general, but I do not think it is ambiguous in the way support is. One can classify actions into or out of this set without too much difficulty. The difficulty arises with the phrase "is the process of." That is as minimal a definition of structure as is possible. About all this tells us is that one should look for a sequence of actions, that is, a process is not a single action. A lot of energy has been expended on describing the individuals who have been successful and the actions they took and that others took along the way to their success. But no structure has emerged. We are thus left with description. Without some element of structure it does not do much good to be able to sort actions into classes and describe those acts.

I conclude that what is missing in these cases, and others as well, is the element of structure. We do a reasonable job of identifying and describing, but we do not seem to know how to look for or find structure.

Let me conclude by addressing the "hopeless" question: How does one get from particulars to principles? The common theme running through the first four sections is that the relationship between particulars and principles is not one of empirical generalization. In this section I have argued that at least one of the missing elements is structure. I would like to suggest a way to look for structure which is mildly heretical, given my "research camp" background. Structure is more likely to be found by examining individual particulars in depth than by looking at lots of particulars in general. I am really trying to answer the question, What sparks an idea? And I do not believe that there is any one answer to that question. But we have tried looking for generalizations, and that has not produced structure. Perhaps looking at particulars "in the right way" will be more productive. "The right way" is with an eye to seeing them as instances of a "principle by which different things are related to each other as just so many forms of one substrata."

DESCRIPTIONS ARE ACCURATE.
PRINCIPLES ARE . . .

How can it happen that descriptions and theories, which are as different as they are, can be brought together? This is the question to be dealt with in this section, but before trying to give some kind of answer to that question I should be quite specific about the ways in which I believe descriptions and organizing principles are importantly different.

A description is a statement or a set of statements about something. A description points beyond itself to some phenomenon about which it purports to give an account. Because it points to specific phenomena, a description is indexed in time and space. Thus, a description is limited in its generality. We know how to evaluate descriptions; they are more or less accurate. Accuracy has two components: One is correspondence, and the other is precision. A description is said to be accurate when the characterization given in the description corresponds to the phenomenon. "This apple is red" is a more or less accurate statement, depending on what we mean by "apple," "is," and "red" and the apple itself.

However, a description may be deemed less rather than more accurate if it is insufficiently precise for our purpose. For example, two astronomers recently investigated the physical makeup of two meteorites. Through microscopic examination they were able to determine qualities that were not otherwise known about the two meteorites, and this led to important speculations about the origin of our solar system. Previous descriptions of the meteorites did not suffer a lack of correspondence, but they were insufficiently precise to reveal the qualities the two astronomers take to be most important about the meteorites.

All of this makes description appear to be quite straightforward, but, of course, it is not. The description of any phenomenon is potentially infinite. This potential must be bounded, and usually this is accomplished because of the purpose of the describer. Notice that this also implies that the criteria to be used in determining the accuracy of a description must be bounded—presumably by the same intentions as used to bound the description. This is an important caveat in characterizing description, but it is one that can be accepted in the context of answering the question of this section.

A theory is a set of statements. Like a description, a theory points beyond itself to some phenomenon about which it purports to give an account. Also, a theory must be bounded. As with description the theoretical possibilities are infinite, and the bounding of this potential is accomplished through the purpose of the theorist just as description is bounded by the purpose of the describer. Unlike a description, the set of phenomena to which the theory points is not bounded by time and space. An organizing principle is general. Finally, the criteria for evaluating a theory must be stated. There is a good deal less agreement on what these criteria should be, and I will suggest only three for consideration here.

First, a theory is simple. Unfortunately, no one has been able to give a general and satisfactory definition of simplicity when applied to theories. It is not that nothing can be said, but rather that there is no mechanical means of specifying that one theory is simpler than another. Thus, it is left up to human beings to make that judgment.

Second, a theory is good if it leads us to expect something and that something turns out to be true. The something may have occurred in the past, in which case, like the astronomers, we look for present traces of its having occurred. The something may occur in the present, in which case we have only to observe to determine if it occurs. Finally, it may occur if we manipulate a situation in an appropriate way. We call this experimentation.

Third, a theory is good if it is fecund. Theories are often defined as a set of axioms and the theorems that can be deduced from them. One should note that it is not necessary that the axioms and theorems be mathematicized for this characterization to be applied. If one accepts this characterization, then the fecundity of the axioms is an important characteristic of the theory. Assuming the other two criteria are met by two theories, the one that gives the greatest number of deductions is judged better.

Remember that Poiseuille's Law was characterized as a valid simplification, and that really is the point of organizing principles. Every occurrence when considered in its fullness is unique, but we need simplifications if we are to cope with the ever-shifting world. But how can a valid simplification become an accurate description? This puzzle, the relationship between generality and particularity, has been with us since the inception of Western civilization, and there are many layers of answers. The answer I want to give is internal to scientific activity, and comes in two parts.

Another Use of Model

Models, particularly mathematical models, are increasingly popular in the social sciences. As we are learning a little mathematics, they are popping up all over the place. We use the word "model" in a particular way. Normally, one begins with a verbal description and then identifies individual parts of this description with parts of a mathematical equation. This yields an equation or a set of equations that can be manipulated with appropriate mathematical tools in hopes of saying something that was not immediately obvious from the initial description. In addition, we often identify the variables in the equation with some empirical data to test the empirical appropriateness of the mathematical equations to a given situation.

Mathematical logicians use the word "model" in a rather different way, and I would like to explicate that use as preparation for part of the answer to how organizing principles may become accurate descriptions. The easiest way to specify how mathematical logicians use "model" is by illustration. Boolean algebra and some of its models will be used, and I will follow Susanne Langer's presentation in this section.

The first step is the definition of an algebra. Langer (1967: 207) defines an algebra in the following way: "A symbolic language for the generalized expression of operations on a set of elements is an algebra." Boolean algebra is such a symbolic language. The set of elements and operations of Boolean algebra are K(a, b, c . . .)$\oplus$$\otimes$=. One of the distinctive characteristics of Boolean algebra is that the elements of the set, K(a, b, c . . .), may take only one of two values. The laws that govern the operations +, ×, = are given by a set of ten primitive propositions or premises. Since the basic premises are not required here, they will not be presented.

As presented here, Boolean algebra is a completely abstract theory. There is no interpretation of the elements, operations, or ten primitive propositions beyond that summarized very briefly above. It is possible, however, to elaborate the theory in many different ways given these elements and operations. And understanding how that is done will serve a useful illustrative purpose in showing how the word "model" is used in mathematics.

I would like to illustrate the following definition of model by using the Boolean algebra briefly characterized above:

Suppose then that L is an informal theory. An assignment of meaning to the primitive terms of L is called an interpretation of L.

If the entity made up of the meaningful versions of the primitive terms of L, as specified by an interpretation of L, satisfies the axioms of L, it is called a model of L [Stoll, 1961: 131].

A model is an interpretation of a theory that satisfies the axioms of the theory. Is there such a model of Boolean algebra? Yes, there are a number of them.

The propositional calculus is one model of Boolean algebra. The elements (P, Q, R . . .) are primitive or unanalyzed propositions. These elements take the values of true or false. Thus, they are two-valued. Langer uses "or" (symbolized by "v") and "and" (symbolized by ".") to interpret $\oplus$ and $\otimes$. In addition, the axioms of Boolean algebra are satisfied when used as the axioms of the propositional calculus. Thus, the propositional calculus is a model or one example of a Boolean algebra.

Set theory can also be constructed as a model of Boolean algebra. In this case the elements of the theory are sets that are two-valued, since an element is either a member of the set or not. The operations $\oplus$ and $\otimes$ are identified with union and intersection, and the axioms of Boolean algebra are satisfied by set theory.

There are a number of other models of Boolean algebra. It can be reconstructed as an algebra operating on the numbers 0 and 1. This yields an algebra that is rather different from the more familiar algebra of real numbers, but it is a realization or model of the Boolean algebra. Directed graphs can be "reconstructed" as a Boolean algebra. The only apparent limit on the models of Boolean algebra is the imagination of man.

It is not necessary to stop at this level of abstraction in developing models of Boolean algebra. The propositional calculus, for example, might itself have a model. The elements of the propositional calculus (P, Q, R . . .) represent any propositions, but if one assigned specific meaning to the elements, one would then have a model of the propositional calculus as long as the axioms of the system were satisfied. For example, assign the following meanings:

EC represents the contribution of a group to a political leader's obtaining or maintaining office.

W   represents the ability of a group to obtain the political action that
     it desires.
GS   represents the size of the group.
GC   represents group cohesion.
WP   represents the ability of the group to obtain the political action
     that it desired in the past.
K   represents the ability of the group to maintain the advantages
     achieved through past political action.

Now three axioms can be added to the basic set of ten axioms:

   (11) $EC \rightarrow W$
   (12) $(GS \cdot GC) \rightarrow EC$
   (13) $(\sim WP \vee \sim K) \rightarrow GC$

The axioms of Boolean algebra are still satisfied, since these
three axioms are all consistent with that axiom set. What
axioms 11, 12, and 13 do is limit the Boolean algebra by giving
three propositions that are assumed to be true and thereby
denying any statements that could be made in the more general
Boolean algebra that are inconsistent with these three propositions. Now one has a model of the calculus of propositions that
might be called a theory of group politics. This is a truncated
model of the propositional calculus, since it does not specify
the conditions under which EC, W, GS, GC, WP, and K will be
true or false and it has limited the propositions that can be
derived, but with these exceptions it is a model of the propositional calculus.

The model of the propositional calculus developed in the
above paragraph may itself have a model. If one replaces every
reference to groups by "labor movement in the United States
between approximately 1920 and 1979," and political leaders
with "nationally elected officials," then one would have a
model of this group theory of politics—a model that directly
applies to a particular group at a particular time and place. If
you would like to know what comes out of this model of group
politics, I commend this chapter's appendix to you.

By now the point of all of this should be coming into focus. By model, mathematical logicians mean a more concrete realization or interpretation of a more general theory. In the Boolean algebra K (a, b, c, ...) can be anything as long as it is two-valued. In the propositional calculus they can be anything that is a proposition, and the two values are true and false.

It is now possible to specify one part of the answer to how theories that are general can become descriptions that are particular. Each of the proposition variables, EC, W, GS, GC, WP, and K, stands for a set of propositions. The phrases "EC represents ...," "GS represents ...," and the rest are very informal rules for defining these sets of propositions. The propositions in these sets may be indexed in time and space. Thus, by choosing the appropriate members of the respective sets, one is able to move from the theory to description. Hence, a theory "becomes" a description by taking the description as a model of the theory. At least that is one way to use model.

Before turning to the second part of the answer to the question of this section, I would like to return to Langer's definition of an organizing principle. Remember that an organizing principle does two things. First, it provides a definition that reduces incommensurables to commensurables. Second, it provides a structure that operates across the defined set of elements. Does the little theory given above do these two things? First, it defines a political situation. There are politicians and there are groups. The politicians want office, and the groups want particular actions. The ability of the groups to obtain the political actions they want is dependent on their abilities to contribute to the aspirations of the political leaders. Also, in defining this situation it yields a structure operating over the sets that have been defined. One might say that the structure is axioms 11 through 13, except that the operations embodied in these axioms depend on the first ten axioms. Thus, the whole thing is the structure; including the restriction to two values. From all of this follow some results that I find rather nice. Moreover, both elements of the definition of an organizing principle are there.

Accurate Descriptions

The world is a complicated place; there can be no gainsaying that. But theories are thought to be good when they are simple and less good the more complicated they are. How, then, can one use a simple theory to describe a complicated phenomenon? One answer is that the structure that produces the complicated consequences is itself simple. This answer has been successful often enough that it has to be taken seriously. The trouble with the answer, however, is that it is partial; something more is needed.

The connection between simple organizing principles and accurate descriptions is to be found in what may be called auxiliary conditions. With the exception of ceteris paribus, auxiliary conditions are much too little noted in characterizing theories. This is the real benefit of the characterization of Poiseuille's Law reported in the first section of this chapter. The assumptions that must hold for Poiseuille's Law to be an accurate description are carefully outlined. We know what must be true for this valid simplification to be an accurate description. The assumptions or auxiliary conditions are explicitly stated. If one of them does not hold, then Poiseuille's Law will no longer be an accurate description, and something must be done to it—making it less simple—to make it an accurate description.

I believe that most of us in what I earlier called the research camp of political science would agree with the above paragraph. However, I find little writing about auxiliary conditions or the same thing under some other name, and I find little research aimed at establishing auxiliary conditions. Thus, I conclude that our understanding of what auxiliary conditions are and the role they play in linking theory and description is minimal. In order to reinforce the importance of auxiliary conditions, I would like to illustrate what they might look like in some political situations.

Before proceeding to the political illustration, I must say something more about the theory of governing which will serve as the basis of this example. First, there is an outcome variable which will be represented by 0. This outcome variable is determined by an environmental complex which will be represented by E. Depending on E, the outcome variable will display a range of behavior. Governing is reducing the variety in the behavior of 0, that is, governing is constraining the behavior of 0 to some subset of the range that would occur if 0 were only dependent on E.

Conant (1969) has shown, in a very general argument, that the ability of the regulator to constrain 0 to a subset of its potential behavior is bounded by the information R has about E. Thus, he has demonstrated for quite general conditions that regulation is bounded by information. This is not, however, the only constraint on the capacity of R to regulate 0. Thus, two things can be concluded. For any level of information R has about E, there is an upper limit on the regulation of 0. For example, if information is minimal or nonexistent, then the amount of regulation is minimal. If information is increased, then R may be able to increase its capability to constrain the behavior of 0. This principle—regulation is bounded by information—will be used in the political example that follows.

However, there is an important condition that must be met for this principle to hold. The environmental complex must be independent of the actions of the regulator. This will be the auxiliary condition in the example to follow.

The international steel business has been in something of a state of transition for more than a decade. It is no longer the case that one or a few countries dominate the world production of steel, and new countries keep entering the production business all of the time. This poses problems, and they are problems that very quickly get politicized. In order to remind you of recent occurrences in this sector of world economics and world politics, I quote part of an editorial in the *Washington Post* (1978a):

> In an attempt to control steel imports, the Carter administration last spring imposed a system known as trigger pricing. As usual, the remedy turns out to have unexpected effects. Since steel remains the largest and most difficult of the import issues, it's worth keeping an eye on the way things seem to be working out.

The American steel companies' central complaint has been that foreign producers are subsidized by governments that, to avoid unemployment, are prepared to sell at heavy losses. When several American mills closed down a year ago, the Carter administration reluctantly decided that it had to do something about the scale of foreign imports. The trick was to protect the American companies from cut-throat pricing, without protecting them from the salutary pressure of legitimate competition from abroad. The solution, rather elegant in concept, was the trigger pricing system. The Treasury was to calculate the true production costs of steel made by the most efficient producers—that is, the Japanese—and publish the figures. Any foreign source offering steel below those prices would be deemed to be selling at a loss and would invite Treasury prosecution for dumping.

When the trigger prices went into effect last May, steel imports dropped. But then in midsummer they started rising again. That's the reason for the current rising volume of protest from the American industry. But the odd thing is that nobody seems to know where all of this steel is going. Despite the higher imports, the production and sales from American mills are holding up very nicely. Imports plus domestic production add up to much more steel than the country is using. Evidently a tremendous buildup of inventories is taking place. What's going on?

A hint: Since the beginning of the year, the value of the yen has been rising rapidly. Since the trigger prices are based on Japanese costs, they follow the yen upward. That means, first of all, that the trigger price schedules haven't been as much of a restraint on inflation in American steel prices as the administration had hoped. But there's more to it. The trigger prices are recalculated every three months. Each revision raises the value of steel in inventory. Buying and holding steel has become, it seems, a safe and easy way to speculate on the decline of the dollar.

Eventually, of course, the speculators will sell these inventories. If it happens suddenly, it will have a drastic effect on American production. The prospect makes the American companies deeply apprehensive. Trigger pricing is providing far less assurance of stability in the steel markets than its authors had hoped.

This is a fascinating story of regulation that has developed a hitch. But in order to make use of it, I will first have to translate it into the framework on governing explicated earlier.

The outcome variable is the price at which steel is being sold in the United States. The Carter administration wanted to regulate this price "to protect the American companies from cut-throat pricing, without protecting them from the salutary pressure of legitimate competition from abroad." The environmental complex is all of those factors that affect the price at which steel is being sold. One major component of this environment is the productive capacity for steel manufacturing in other countries. The Carter administration did not want to affect the productive capacity of other countries. It only wanted to regulate the price at which that productive capacity was put on the market. Thus, E is or should be independent of R.

The basic mechanism was already in place, that is, there is a law against dumping or selling below cost by foreign steel companies. The problem was information. How does the U.S. government know when dumping is occurring? Prior to the spring of 1978 someone had to notice that steel from some country was selling at a very low rate and bring this to the attention of the Treasury Department. The Treasury Department then had to find out what it cost to produce the steel, and then go into court and present this evidence of illegal behavior. It was a long and contentious process. According to the U.S. steel manufacturers, regulation was severely bounded by information. They contended that there was quite a lot of dumping going on, but not much regulation, because of the difficulty of proving that the dumping was actually that. Then came the trigger price. The Treasury Department had to compute the cost of producing steel in only one country. They do this quarterly, and publish the results. Any steel offered for sale below that price is assumed to be dumping, and regulation can begin very quickly.

The situation was that regulation was bounded by information. The trigger price mechanism substantially improved the information from E to R. Thus, the law against dumping could be brought to bear, and regulation should have become more effective. But, at least in the short run, things did not work out exactly as expected. The steel industry contended that they were still threatened with economic disaster. Is this an instance that runs counter to the principle that regulation is bounded by information? That would be a threatening conclusion, since a single counterinstance is sufficient to deny a principle that is claimed to be general. I believe that it is not a counterinstance, and the reason that it is not is that the auxiliary condition was not met in this case.

The principle holds when E is independent of R, but notice what happened in this case. The United States set the trigger price in terms of the cost of production in Japan. This happened at just the time the yen was appreciating sharply against the dollar. This created a new use for steel: speculation on the decline of the dollar. Thus, steel was bought to be stored and sold at some future date. When that date comes it will dramatically drive the price of steel out of the range the government desired. U.S. steel companies view this prospect with great alarm. From our point of view, it is a hitch in a particular regulatory mechanism. From their point of view, it is economic hardship if not a disaster. However, one views the prospect, it is surely an anticipation of failure of regulation to keep the price of steel within the desired range. But this comes about because E is not independent of R. Thus, the auxiliary condition is not met.

By recognizing that the auxiliary condition is not met, we can understand why our expectation based on the principle is not met. We can also anticipate that when the dollar-yen ratio becomes stable again, this "hitch" will no longer operate, and the trigger price mechanism may, in the long run, turn out to be very helpful in regulating the price of steel. It does dramatically increase information, and thus unbounds the regulatory effectiveness of antidumping laws.

The steel-dumping example is not normal political science, so let me turn to an example for which there is at least some community of scholars in political science working on the problem. For the sake of argument, let us assume that Richardson's (1960) arms-race model is a true principle. Richardson suggested that the change in the arms of two nations might be understood in terms of the threat each nation felt because of the arms of the other nation, the economic constraints imposed by past arms acquisitions by each nation, and the general level of hostility that the nations feel toward each other. If we take this to be a true principle, then we should be immediately led to ask what are the auxiliary conditions necessary to convert this principle into an accurate description. I will discuss several; some of them have been investigated and some may not have been.

One assumption of the theory as it is usually presented is that threat, economic constraints, and hostility are unchanging. This is the simplest way to state the principle, but it seems to me implausible as a description of any two nations over an extended period of time. Thus, it seems that one should look for auxiliary conditions that would indicate when to expect threat, economic constraints, and hostility to be constant, and when to expect them to change. This is something more than just asking if they have changed in any given arms race, although that would surely be part of what needed to be done. It would involve looking for conditions necessary to guarantee constancy and change.

A second assumption of the theory is that neither nation acts in order to induce the other nation to act in a specific way. Arms races are not games of strategy. But this condition may not always be met. The first step is determining if there are nations that act (as opposed to talk) as though they are involved in a game. But the ultimate objective of this work would be to discover the auxiliary condition that specifies when a nation will act to induce certain kinds of behavior on the part of the other nation and when a nation will not act this way.

A third assumption of the principle is that arms races take place between two nations. But the United States blew a bundle in the war in Vietnam, and surely only part of that could be attributed to its arms race with the Soviet Union. Thus, one needs an auxiliary condition that stipulates when this simplifying assumption is appropriate and when it is not. And if one wants accurate description, one needs, as in the other cases above, a method for taking into account the effects of the auxiliary condition not being met.

More illustrations could be given, but I hope that this is enough to make the point. The point is that simple theories are accurate descriptions only under very special circumstances. An important part of both developing a theory and of using it to characterize something that is actually occurring is getting the auxiliary conditions straight. Without the auxiliary conditions the theory may be simple, but it will not be an accurate description of much of what happens. This leads me to two more points that need to be made before concluding this section.

First, simple theories are in a very important way the product of a particular way of thinking about the world. If a simple theory is an accurate description only under special conditions, then when the conditions change the theory must change. What, then, leads one to say that those conditions that make the simple theory an accurate description are primary and everything else is secondary? How does one justify relegating most of what happens to the limbo of special conditions? Since I have participated for some time in a discipline that takes accuracy of description as the sine qua non of success, I marvel at the temerity of those who can say that simplicity is the goal. I conclude that this difference is largely a matter of preference, habit, and training. Most of what happens is relegated to the status of a special case, because that is the way science is done.

Second, one of the reactions to the point of view that I have articulated in this section is that we would be able to accomplish this only if we had laboratories—that laboratories are necessary for this kind of theorizing. I do not believe that this is the case, and I would like to indicate why. It seems to me that a laboratory is first and perhaps foremost a way of thinking. To use a laboratory effectively you have to think, "Under conditions 1, 2, and 3, if x then y." But that way of thinking is not necessarily restricted to the laboratory. The world is a rich storehouse of events occurring under different conditions. I am not even convinced that, except for mostly trivial cases, it is easier to exercise control in a laboratory than it is to find control exercised in the world. Large laboratories are costly and difficult to build, and they are costly and difficult to control. The real key is the way of thinking, and that involves finding instances for which conditions 1, 2, and 3 are true and then determining whether "if x then y" is true. The major advantage that I see to laboratories is the ease with which the scientific community can repeat research. The laboratory scientist does not have to wait around for the world to produce a special set of conditions again but can produce them once again in the laboratory.

How does an organizing principle that is both simple and general become an accurate description? This is the principle question addressed in this section, and the answer has been twofold. First, an organizing principle becomes particular when a particular set of occurrences are taken as a model of the theory. Here "model" is used in a specific but easily defined way. Second, accuracy in description is given by the auxiliary conditions that specify what conditions must hold for the theory to be an accurate description and how the theory must be changed to be accurate under other conditions.

THE RIGHT SORT OF
ORGANIZING PRINCIPLE

I have read a good deal of philosophy of science, and I believe that most of what I have written here is consistent with arguments that are rather generally accepted. So what is the point? The point is that I could not figure out how to convert what I read into political science, and when I looked around at the discipline I did not find much assistance in making the conversion. Thus, the point is not so much the conclusions as it is the trip. I want to know what the right sort of law would look like when the phenomena explained are political and not sticky liquids.

Having made the trip, I think that I have a better idea about what a theory of some political phenomenon would look like and how it might become an accurate description. I hope you are also in the same position.

I leave you with the briefest of summaries of the conclusions. They are not the trip, but they are where the trip has ended for me.

What is an organizing principle that it may order particulars? It is that by which apparently incommensurable things are "related to each other as just so many forms of one substrata."

How may an organizing principle that is both simple and general become an accurate description? By taking particular occurrences as a model of the theory, and with the aid of auxiliary conditions.

APPENDIX

Victory and Defeat,

or

How Can One Explain What Happened to That Old Curmudgeon, George Meany

Here is the empirical observation (taken from *The Washington Post*) that motivates this flight into theorizing.

Two years ago (November, 1976) AFL-CIO President George Meany could look up and down Pennsylvania Avenue from his imposing headquarters on 16th Street and see political IOUs sprouting from every crack.

Eight years of Republican drought were ending, and organized labor was ready to reap the harvest of the Democratic administration and lopsidedly Democratic Congress that it was helping to elect. By Labor Day 1978, the unions' most ambitious legislative program since the New Deal would be well on its way to enactment.

But it didn't turn out quite that way.

The program now lies crumpled in a congressional dustbin. Jimmy Carter and George Meany are periodically snapping at each other across Lafayette Park. And union leaders are claiming that the "radical right," bankrolled from corporate profits, is out to get the entire labor movement.

Dashed expectations are commonplace in politics, but what happened to the labor movement and their program is 1977-1978 exceeds the norm by a very great distance. How is one to account for the debacle which labor's program became? I will begin by constructing an argument about what it takes to win in the policymaking process. Then this argument will be reexamined to shed light on the current plight of the unions.

Politicians want to be elected and reelected. Thus, electoral prospects are never very far below the surface in political debate and the machinations that produce policy. This leads to a fundamental principle of American politics: If a group makes a substantial contribution to electoral outcomes, then it is most likely to win its policy objectives. By letting EC represent "substantial contribution to electoral outcome," this proposition can be abbrevaited in the following way:

EC then Win   [1]

This, of course, is the assumption of the first two paragraphs of the newspaper story quoted.

Elections are won with votes, and a group that has a lot of voters is in a good position to make a significant contribution to electoral outcomes. But size by itself is not enough. The voters must be mobilized to vote in a specific way, and that requires group cohesion. These two factors are necessary for making a difference in elections. Letting GS represent "group size" and GC represent "group cohesion," this condition can be abbrevaited as follows:

(GS and GC) then EC   [2]

Group cohesion is, no doubt, a function of many things, but among the politically relevant factors are that there is something the group wants and that it either has not been able to win it in the past or has not been able to hold on to it. Nothing stimulates group activity like not being able to obtain something it wants or, once having obtained it, then losing it. Letting WP represent "won in the past" and K represent "keep what was won in the past," this proposition can be abbreviated by

(not WP or not K) then GC   [3]

With this third proposition the general structure of the argument is complete. They are listed together for easy reference.

EC then Win   [1]
if (GS and GC) then EC   [2]
if (not WP or not K) then GC   [3]

With two auxiliary pieces of information and this general argument it is possible to account for labor's rise in political influence. First, the labor movement grew rapidly during the 1920s, '30s, '40s, and '50s. It became a group of substantial size; thus, GS. During this same period the labor movement developed a rather long list of rights and benefits that it wanted but was unable to achieve without political assistance; thus, not WP. Now for the deductions.

EC then Win   [1]
if (GS and GC) then EC   [2]
if (not WP or not K) then GC   [3]

GS   [4]
not WP   [5]

not WP or not K   /5 add.   [6]
GC   /3,6 Modus Ponens   [7]
GS and GC   /7,4 Conj.   [8]
EC   /2,8 Modus Ponens   [9]

Win   /1,9 Modus Ponens   [10]

Thus resulted policy favored by labor, the headquarters over-looking the White House, and a prominent place in American politics.

But 1977-1978 was not a good time for the labor movement, and not much light has been shed on that by this argument. Let us use propositions 1 through 4, since the labor movement had declined only slightly from its peak membership by 1976, and "not Win something" can be adduced from the current plight of the labor movement.

EC then Win		[1]
if (GS and GC) then EC		[2]
if (not WP or not K) then GC		[3]
GS		[4]
not Win		[5]
not EC	/1,5 Modus Tollens	[6]
not (GS and GC)	/2,6 Modus Tollens	[7]
not GS or not GC	/7 DeMorgan	[8]
not GC	/8,4 Disj. Syllogism	[9]
not (not WP or not K)	/3,9 Modus Tollens	[10]
WP and K	/10 DeMorgan	[11]

A group that does not win has won in the past and has been able to hold on to those victories. The moral of this tale is, "Victory carries with it the seeds of defeat."

Lest you think this argument applies only to the labor movement, I quote part of William Raspberry's description of the 1975 annual meeting of the NAACP.

And yet looking back on the week of June 30-July 4, I can't get rid of the feeling that: nothing happened. Nor is that by any means a unique view of what Executive Director Roy Wilkens described as a "highly successful" convention.

That subject (whether Wilkens would resign) could not have commanded stage center, however, if there had been talk of new plans and strategies for dealing with racial problems in America, of rearranging old political alliances or forming major new ones or any of the other things that used to convey the feeling of activism.

But that was the talk of the days when the problem was to get rid of segregationist laws, to litigate against Jim Crow practices, to end harassment of black voters and to enact civil rights legislation.

The NAACP was so successful at attacking those problems that hardly any work of that sort remains to be done. . . .

It was a good deal easier, and cheaper, when all it had to do was to feed problems into the system and let the law take over.

Maybe that's the price of progress [Washington Post, 1975].

I reflect on the recent gains of blacks: the Bakke decision, the passage of the Humphrey-Hawkins bill, and others.

NOTE

1. There is, of course, no such thing as a "typical" political scientist. We are all over the intellectual map. This is a caricature of the empiricist tradition, which is used to make a point. It is, however, not difficult to find reports of research activity that look much like this picture.

REFERENCES

Conant, R. (1969) "The information transfer required in regulatory processes." *IEEE Transactions on System Science and Cybernetics* (October).
Langer, S. (1953) *An Introduction to Symbolic Logic* (2nd ed.). New York: Dover.
——— (1967) *An Introduction to Symbolic Logic* (3rd ed.). New York: Dover.
Richardson, L. F. (1960) *Arms and Insecurity.* Pittsburgh: Boxwood Press.
Slater, J. C. and N. H. Prank (1933) *Introduction to Theoretical Physics.* New York: McGraw-Hill.
Stoll, R. R. (1961) *Sets, Logic and Axiomatic Theories.* San Francisco: Freeman.
Tuchinsky, P. (1978) *Viscous Fluid Flow and the Integral Calculus,* UMAP.
Washington Post (1975) July 9: A-15.
Washington Post (1978a) October 7: A-18.
Washington Post (1978b) November 11: A-11.
Washington Post (1978c) November 21: D-9, D-10.
Washington Post (1978d) November 27: A-3.

3

The Historical Nature of
Social-Scientific Knowledge

The Case of
Comparative Political Inquiry

ROGER BENJAMIN

A retreat to the position that systematic generalizations about social and political phenomena are impossible is unwarranted. Equally unwarranted is the position that ignores the fact that individuals, groups, institutions, and societies exist within a constantly changing contextual rubric. This chapter seeks to show that political inquiry is a fundamentally historical enterprise. By history (context) I mean the groups, institutions, language, culture, and macrosocietal environments within which humans think and act. We should, of course, develop and apply methods and techniques of analysis to political phenomena as rigorously as possible. However, the actual phenomena we study, describe, and model are in constant flux.

During periods of relative social-economic and political stability, social scientists are lured into a false sense of security regarding the ahistorical validity of empirical generalizations. The power of a research program in social science may appear to cumulate within a particular historical context (defined as any period in which stability is more dominant than change in society). Inevitably, new problems and basic social-economic and political change reach a threshold point. Change occurs of such magnitude as to require a wholesale alteration in the *way* social and political phenomena are to be studied.

One may distinguish between two types of change. With Cortes et al. (1974), one may speak of dynamics, or the temporal variations within the boundaries of a particular system (context). Conversely, one may postulate diachronic change, that is, change in the fundamental structure of a system. I shall argue that, within a particular system, the study of dynamics may proceed on the basis of a relatively stable view of the world. Here one sees periods of "normal" science development. However, when diachronic change occurs, the fundamental need is to reconceptualize the underlying processes that produce such change. Even within a major historical period, much change of a systemic nature occurs. A large task for social scientists is to determine whether system change is really only surface noise or of a diachronic nature.

When historical change of a diachronic nature occurs, strategy of inquiry questions becomes especially crucial. By "strategy of inquiry" I mean the *way* one puts the various building blocks of the logic of inquiry together—for example, whether one emphasizes problem formulation, theory development, or reconceptualization, or whether one focuses on measurement and data analysis (Benjamin, 1980). When diachronic change occurs, new research programs are formulated and new theories developed (Lakatos, 1970). Scholarship is most exciting, though perplexing. To disaggregate and replace theories and models that have been the productive underpinnings of research in the past is a difficult task.

In the wake of World War II, for example, American political science developed on the foundations of the pluralist conceptualization of politics and spawned the behaviorial revolution in the study of political phenomena. The pluralist research program developed an important body of work. Social science, however, is an applied field of human activity. We must work hard to keep up with historical change. As we move into the

1980s, I believe we are in another period of diachronic change. Such a change in the structure of social-economic and political systems requires us to be open to new ways to formulate theoretical questions. I shall attempt to justify these assertions in the sections that follow.

I shall not argue here that we should abandon scientific method in political inquiry. My aim is to construct a position that treats methodology as important but subsidiary to theory. By theory I shall mean, only, general intellectual principles with which one interprets particular dimensions of the "real" world. With examples from political science, economics, and especially comparative politics, I shall suggest that Mannheim's view of social change remains valid.

We are indeed faced with a fundamental paradox: Social-economic and political processes change; they form multiple continua that often appear to move in concert in ways that also appear systematic. Social scientists attempt to model these changes. Common conceptual referents, for example, are taken to capture the process of modernization. Within benchmarks, such as tradition and modernity, we develop an entire body of literature, some of it approaching reasonable standards of rigor defined by recent agreed-upon cannons of political methodology. However, virtually as soon as we begin to achieve some success in apprehending an important political process, diachronic change occurs in such fields as modernization to render our models obsolete.

Some would argue this means that much of the scientific claims for the temporal content of social-scientific knowledge are invalidated. I shall only assert here that much merit remains in using and extending the apparatus of techniques and methods developed in political science over the past thirty years. Moreover, in comparative politics, as in politics and economics itself, the evidence of diffusion of industrial, political-communication, educational, and other common patterns is unmistakable. There seems to be merit in assuming common processes of social-economic and political change, even if that particular common-process model appears flawed.

If by theory one means deductive-nomological architecture designed to stand *across* historical periods, the prospects are dim. A more useful position, I shall argue, is to take seriously the view of much of social science as a fundamentally historical enterprise. If the discussion that follows is persuasive, the strategy suggestions that follow may be useful. Certainly the most general suggestion highlighted is the importance of placing one's research in a broader historical context.

STRATEGY VERSUS METHODOLOGY

Elsewhere I have argued that the special claims for a comparative (cross-national) methodology are unwarranted (Benjamin, 1980). All comparative methods are really some variant of experimental, statistical, or comparable case approaches found in all areas of political science and social science more generally. Comparative political inquiry shall mean here political studies that take as their aim the development of cross-system (usually cross-national), cross-time, and cross-level generalizations. The largest body of work is, of course, centered in cross-system studies. If the claims about comparative methodology are unwarranted, we must justify comparative research on some other basis. What unites comparativists is the assumption that processes of organized complexity are variable across systems, levels, and time. One need not assume one uniform curve along which all societies (or parts thereof) move. Rather, comparativists assume that comparative research presents more variation to check, extend, or reject within-system-based findings. By implication, this means that comparativists assume that single within-system designs capture only one system structure among many that exist along multiple continua among and within the many social systems that exist across systems, levels, and time.

Ironically, this process assumption presents us with a variant of the Mannheim paradox, forming arguments at once for and against theorizing about social phenomena in their various forms. As soon as we create a model, a representation of the structure within which some process occurs, we must be aware of the fact that the model may be static, not dynamic: For many social scientists, priority is given to the realization of "theory"—any explanatory system that is reliable throughout space and time. Yet if the development of society transcends epochs and specific historical periods labeled feudalism or, more recently, industrialization, then the quest for explanations that endure across diachronic change becomes problematic.

The one thing that virtually everyone agrees on is that social systems are complex, multivariant, and potentially unstable. The lesson from Brunner and Liepelt (1972) remains apt: Cross-sectional statistical studies—in the absence of theories that permit predictions of the *precise* way (strength, direction, order) variables in the described system relate to one another— typically assume the *stability* of the relationships across time. This is a risky assumption. However, what does comparative research buy in the absence of a deductive theory of political change that allows one to juxtapose the units being compared? The answer must be equally pessimistic. If the linear positive relationships discovered in the United States between urbaniza- tion and voter turnout are found to be negative in many local and national polities, it may be due to the fact that these units are at different and unknown points in the process of political change. Przeworski and Teune's (1970) call for most-similar and most-different designs was a step forward because it sensitized comparativists to a host of methodological and technique issues. Unfortunately, efforts like theirs have kept our attention away from the more fundamental questions relating to theory.

Research designs are not a substitute for *theory* development, that is, the effort to articulate general structuring principles with which to guide and structure the world around us. Theo- ries, concepts, and explanations may themselves be developed through the standard categories of the logic of inquiry. Thus, a theory is more or less inductive or deductive, parsimonious, complete, or powerful. Strategy is a different matter, because the *choice* of modes of inquiry is itself a historical question. Which portion of the logic of inquiry to focus on—from assump- tions, problem formulation, and definition stage *to* concept formation, measurement, and data analysis—is a strategic mat- ter. It is not easy to discuss strategy, because such matters are

closer to the context of discovery than the context of justification. This chapter is based on my assessment that we should be
concerned again with opening up concepts, reworking old questions, developing new puzzles, junking old theories, and developing new ones, rather than developing and applying methodologies.

If one is concerned with a historical period that is relatively
stable, within-system versus across-system research may be useful if applied to comparable cases. However, what does one do
in a period of diachronic threshold change between system-
states? Shall we give up our large investment in scientific political inquiry, or, for example (as appears to be the case with
many economists trained in the neoclassical tradition), continue
to develop our methodological hammers even though the assumptions underlying them appear out of date? At such times it is
important to examine the research programs extant in historical
perspective in order to engage in the strategy of inquiry in the
broadest sense. Let me develop my argument with illustrative
material.

POLITICS, ECONOMICS, AND
COMPARATIVE POLITICAL INQUIRY,
1960 and 1980

The First Context

When I went to graduate school in the early 1960s, consensus
existed among the then-leaders in political science about a
number of important points. First, politics and economics were
viewed as separate enterprises. Of course, it was acknowledged
that there were connections between the economy and the
polity. Lipset (1960), for example, developed his thesis about
the social and economic requisites of democracy. However, the
connection was viewed as benign; political development came to
be equated with democratization and the achievement of
strong, centralized political institutions (Huntington, 1968).
Economic development was viewed as a requisite, and perhaps
determinant, of political development. In domestic and compar-

ative studies, pluralism was articulated as the dominant conceptualization of the role of the state. Under pluralism the state is viewed as the neutral umpire that keeps the rules and enforces fair competition between interest groups in society. The state itself does not take on any structural meaning under pluralism; the state is simply the sum of individual and collective actors (see Lowi, 1979).

During the 1950s the American economy entered its mature industrialization phase. Although the United States had many interests abroad, a clear distinction was maintained between domestic and international affairs. In such a historical period the mood was ripe for theories and models that focused on the system level and assumed stability rather than conflict and change. If it was appropriate to write about the coming "end of ideology," it was also appropriate to wonder whether the United States had reached the apex of development. If we had reached the end of history, then scientific study of politics would yield generalizations that would hold across time. Classical political theory was no longer of anything other than historical interest. (I have placed more detailed discussion on the transition from the 1960s to the 1970s in the appendix to this chapter.) Both the "real" world of the 1950s and early 1960s, and the political science developed to analyze it appear dated. I do not wish to suggest that the best work of the period (Dahl, 1961; Lipset, 1960; Deutsch, 1963; Almond and Powell, 1966) is inferior to subsequent work. Rather, I believe the work of one scholarly generation takes on different meaning and should be read differently as succeeding generations of scholars attempt to apprehend "their" world.

The Current Historical Context

It is time to reconsider basic relationships between politics and economics in the context of the breakdown of the distinction between domestic and comparative/international politics. This breakdown is especially important with respect to relationships between postindustrial and industrial states. It is also time to question and reconceptualize some principal assumptions of neoclassical economics as they relate to domestic and international political economy policy. It is necessary to attack first-order questions such as how one should conceptualize the boundaries between economics and politics. Do we need a wholesale facelift or replacement of neoclassical market-related assumptions? Do government and international-system-generated "exogenous" variables so affect the domestic private economic system of even the largest nation-states as to render the original assumptions obsolete? Let us develop some implications of the "new" constraints for both domestic and international economic and political relationships—within postindustrial societies and between postindustrial and industrial societies.

Statement of the Problem

In political science many scholars have studied domestic (within-system) change where they focus on particularized practices of political culture, institutions and behavior that appear to warrant sustained attention. They look at what is unique, specific to the particular political system, and treat extranational forces as exogenous. In comparison, specialists in comparative and international politics concentrate on common cross-system and and internation patterns of political activity. Disregarding whether these distinctions ever had merit, they are increasingly questioning them today. What political system is even substantially autonomous today? Instantaneous diffusion of new ideas concerning lifestyles, levels of equality and liberty, and conflict and revolution reverberate throughout the world via students returning from abroad, tourism, and the communications media. Moreover, if it is the case that the distinction between the domestic and international economy is breaking down as well, decline of political autonomy follows that breakdown. Let us look at a couple of examples in the economic realm.

Penetration of Economic Economies by International Factors. In economic policy both monetarist and Keynesian solutions to problems such as inflation and unemployment typically assume a closed domestic system. The language of neoclassical economics—supply and demand, economies and diseconomies of scale, and the theory of the firm—is largely applicable to domestic economies. Yet many, if not all, economies are increasingly constrained by international economic activities of multinational corporations, "voluntary and involuntary" trade agreements, OPEC-type cartels, and internation migration of labor. It is virtually impossible, at least in Western countries, for a single country to avoid a generalized recession that develops in the international system. Surely it is time to build in more fully the domestic economic effects of the international economic system.

Macroeconomic Regulation. Keynesian solutions to inflation, unemployment, and economic growth are no longer working well or perhaps at all—at least in Western Europe, the United States, Canada, and Japan. It is now possible to have both high unemployment and inflation. It is also the case that the rate of economic growth is slowest in what many observers consider the most advanced economies. Government policy advisors, political leaders, and economists appear equally at sea. Many economists and other public policy advisors admit the tools to deal with the major economic policy problems of the day are out of date. The intellectual cupboard appears barren of new ideas.

Decline of Industry. A slightly different cluster of problems fall under the heading decline of industry or decline of the manufacturing sector. In the group of societies I have labeled postindustrial, the service sector especially including the public sector dominates the industrial sector. Hence, industry is no longer the main engine of the economy.[1] In these same societies both neo-conservatives and liberal socialists lament the crisis of government, governmental burdens, and societal strain. Economic growth has also slowed to levels far below what these same societies have achieved historically. Moreover, it is in these same societies that productivity increases decline. These issues go together.

The Effect of Changing Comparative Advantage. Coincidentally, it is again in these postindustrial societies that the time-honored agreement on the principle of free trade throughout the international system is under assault. Historically, some of these societies have borne the effects of loss of comparative advantage in industries such as textiles. As we move into the

1980s, however, it is increasingly difficult for political elites in the United States and Great Britain, for example, to ignore the devastating regional consequences of the decline of the auto, steel, and other basic manufacturing industries.

Do Common Principles Underlie These Problems?

What underlying common principles unite or underlie these problems? My view, stated below, is that four apparently distinct, theoretical areas of politics and economics (1) shed considerable light on the four examples of problems stated above, (2) lead to the implication that politics and economics need to be rejoined under the political economy label, and (3) suggest there are a new set of joint domestic and international constraints on the political economy, constraints that not only affect the postindustrial societies, where the effects are more dramatic, but also affect the industrial and Third World states, with whom the postindustrial societies trade. In short, the new constraints, based on the four theories sketched below, suggest the need for a wholesale effort to reconceptualize economics and political science. In these fields the distinction between the domestic and international systems no longer makes sense. Moreover, classical Marxist theories may be unsupple or sterile, but neoclassical models are off the mark as well. Some societies, our postindustrial group, have moved beyond industrialization, "beyond capitalism itself."[2] Next, I turn to a survey of the theory sources.

THE THEORIES: STABLE SOCIETIES AND ECONOMIC DECLINE, THE PRODUCT CYCLE, COLLECTIVE GOODS, AND CRITICAL THEORY IN POSTINDUSTRIAL SOCIETIES

Stable Societies and Economic Decline

Mancur Olson (forthcoming) has developed an intriguing model that explains aspects of the problems noted above through the development of a variant of the logic of collective action thesis Olson developed previously. With respect to Western, pluralist societies, Olson argues that the longer the period of domestic political stability, the greater the propensity of interest groups to form. This is so, he stresses, because once groups attain a reasonable material standard, strong mixes of incentives and sanctions drive individuals into collective-action units of all sorts—unions, business, and trade associations. Individuals perhaps resort to collective action to attain new benefits, but they are more apt to unite for defensive reasons; they seek to protect gains already attained. Olson further demonstrates, in a way familiar to those who know his work (Olson, 1965), that rational behavior for individual collective-action units and what is good for the overall economy may well be different. In fact, over time, entrepreneurial activity and overall, societywide economic growth decline. The economy takes on the appearance of a common pool problem where rigid rules prohibit the movement of capital. Interest-group behavior eventually results in stagnation of economic growth. The model's main points are persuasive. If the model has merit, it is most applicable to the set of postindustrial societies identified above. These societies are where economic growth slowdown is occurring.

A parallel argument to the Olson thesis on the decline of economic growth derives from a paper by the distinguished economist William Baumol (1967). He divides all economic activity into the technically progressive and the technically nonprogressive. Technically progressive activity is that of the familiar marketplace, where the laws of supply and demand and efficiency criteria (from the theory of the firm) operate. Many activities in the public sector are not easily measured by such criteria. In fact, we may well need a new set of criteria to evaluate "progress" in the public sector. Now, if it is also the case that the public sector becomes dominant in postindustrial societies, is it any wonder that economic "growth," as historically measured, declines? Indeed, one distinction between Britain, where economic growth has slowed, and Japan and Germany, where economic growth has risen, is precisely in the relative sizes of their public sectors.

Changing Comparative Advantage
and the Product Cycle

Recent work on the concept of product cycle is relevant to my thesis that the division between the domestic and international dimensions of politics and economics has broken down and must be reconceptualized. The political dimensions of the product-cycle idea have been summarized by James Kurth (1979). The argument is simple in its economic components. Consider the American automobile industry as an example. The automobile is invented and the industry developed largely in the United States (the metropolitan country). Production and, of course, consumption of the automobile grow rapidly in the domestic American market as a function of increased productivity (invention of the assembly line) and lowered cost to consumers. Consumers also enjoy rapidly rising standards of living as the economy grows. In the American case, rapid population growth from the early to the mid-twentieth century provides an increasing pool of consumers as well.

Eventually, the domestic market reaches a point of relative saturation. This is simply to say that there comes a point where rapid growth rates in car sales decline. At this point, especially, the attention of the domestic car manufacturers turns to the international market, where the return of profits is higher and a greater possibility for continued expansion of markets exists. Moreover, in our American-based car example, the industry has comparative advantage over its foreign competitors because of a strong lead in technology, management techniques, and size of production units that contribute to economies of scale. Both profits and increased productivity contribute to the continued contribution of the auto industry toward economic growth of the American economy. This is the period of multinational growth of the American auto industry.

However, apparently a point is reached when automobiles are produced more cheaply and/or made of better quality by foreign competitors. The ability to develop and use technology is not a uniquely American talent. Moreover, the foreign competitor may well generate the ability to produce automobiles at a lower cost because of a lower wage structure. First, the American auto manufacturers lose their comparative advantage in the international markets. Finally, the tables are turned. The foreign auto makers invade and conquer the U.S. market; the product cycle is complete.

Actual cases of product cycles have occurred (or changing comparative advantage) in a variety of industries, electrical equipment, and now automobiles and steel. In every case, the cycle begins in the metropolitan country. Diffusion and export of the technology and industry abroad occur. Finally, the metropolitan country's industry is attacked. In one sense, what I have sketched is nothing more than what free-trade exponents have preached since Adam Smith. In theory, what should happen in the country that originated the product is one or a combination of two alternatives. A by-product or perhaps direct result of economic development is a better educated labor force with greater skills in advanced information system-related areas. The labor force should thus move up to a new set of products— from automobiles and steel to telecommunications, for example. Alternatively, the productivity costs in the metropolitan country will actually fall below the productivity costs in the foreign country. Thus, the auto industry in the United States, for example, would again have the opportunity to attain comparative advantage. I shall draw a series of alternative inferences below. Again, however, the countries losing comparative advantage or at the "end" of the product cycle in many industries are the countries that are currently moving from industrial to postindustrial status.

Postindustrialization, Collective Goods Theory, and Critical Theory

It is always difficult to decide whether it is appropriate to use a new benchmark or continuum when thinking about socio-political change. Poles or benchmarks, such as tradition and modernity or industrial and now postindustrial society, constrain and mask as much as they highlight. It is, however, sensible to use such labels—though always in a provisional sense—to mark apparent threshold changes in the society, economy, and polity. In any event, consensus is growing that it is not "business as usual," and that social-economic and political change beyond the "stages" identified as modernization or industrialization is occurring in Western Europe, North America (minus Mexico), and Japan.

Postindustrialization

Intense debates about the direction and meaning of this change mark each of the social sciences concerned with macro-historical change. It is now possible to draw the threads together into a mosaic that captures some of the emergent changes. In the economic system a point that we might call mature industrialization is defined as the juncture in economic growth where manufacturing or industrial-related activities account for the greatest proportion of the gross national product. The other major areas of economic activity are typically divided into agriculture (primary) or service categories.

However, in a number of Western European countries, and certainly in the United States, industry is no longer the main engine of the economy; rather, the service sector, which includes the public component, increasingly dominates. Much economic activity in the public sector is not easily measurable in terms of its efficiency or actual "technical progressivity." Among the many implications of this changeover are three. First, if many areas in a nation's economic activity are not encompassed by the market, we need new measures of efficiency that go beyond the standard measures of productivity. In the absence of an effective market mechanism actually in place to provide guides for wage increases, the alternative appears to be collective action; citizens in the largest and most powerful unions raid the public treasury. Second, there may well be upper limits to the public sector—in part or in its entirety—because of a declining tax base ravaged by a decline in the industrial base and an increase in inflation. Finally, inflation appears to play an increasing role in the economies of the societies alluded to; perhaps this is due to the first points noted.

These societies appear to be entering an era where both inflation and unemployment require application of the post-Keynesian label. It is not just rising energy costs that fuel inflation. Several postindustrial economies look increasingly similar to what Olson and others call a common pool problem. A tragedy of the commons is created in the absence of market criteria that held down wages and costs in the industrial era. Precious few incentives exist for anyone to hold down wage demands in a postindustrial era. Neoclassical economics was developed to describe and model capitalism, an economic phase associated with industrialization. Perhaps it is time to focus on what economists call nonmarket decision-making models.

These economic changes have parallels in society at large and in the values of its citizens. Population growth and urbanization rise and reach their peak at the mature industrialization phase; thereafter, population growth declines to apparently a zero-growth point. The cities empty as citizens move to the suburbs. Formal education levels reach unprecedented levels. Perhaps because many citizens have achieved an adequate material standard of living, the focus of public policy discussion changes from an emphasis on the quantity of goods produced to the quality of goods and services produced.

This may be a natural evolution. In the nineteenth and twentieth centuries our forefathers worked simply to establish basic social institutions on a societywide level. For example, institutions to deliver minimum social and educational services were founded. Once such institutions are established, however, attention turns to the quality of education and social services delivered. As groups develop a better material base and more leisure time, they naturally become more critical and demanding of services to be tailored to their particular, specialized needs.

More controversial are research findings that indicate substantial value change at the individual level is transforming the belief systems of publics in postindustrial societies (Inglehart, 1977). The argument is that many citizens change values from an emphasis on bourgeois, material wants, such as order and economic security, to self-actualization values, equality, and social-psychological concerns. The increased emphasis on equality translates into demands for greater participation in decision-making. Again, I would add only that there may be a natural evolution connected to this value change similar to the transformation of educational concerns noted. Finally, in discussions of both economic and social change substantial agreement exists that interdependence of all types increases and that information becomes a defining characteristic of the age (Bell, 1973).

The above points guide my thinking about issues and arguments developed by Olson and members of the product-cycle school. However, two additional sets of arguments may be abstracted from different theory traditions, which may be used to interpret basic political implications of the postindustrial sketch. First, there is collective goods theory, developed originally by economists to handle a variety of nonmarket decision-making problems. Second, there is critical theory, developed mainly by European neo-Marxists who are attempting to develop a radical critique of advanced capitalist societies (Habermas, 1973).

Collective goods adherents move from the individual to the group, institutional, and societal levels. Whenever and wherever change is perceived, one looks for the mixture of incentives and sanctions that leads individuals to change their attitudes and behavior. Critical theorists, for their part, operate at the macro-system level and search for the societywide patterns of social-economic and political change. Such changes, they argue, create disjunctures between the state and society, the individual and institutions, disjunctures that dictate wholesale social and political change. The point, unacknowledged by either of these schools, is that their arguments converge to similar points on a number of issues. This convergence supports my argument that politics and economics are facing a new set of constraints in postindustrial societies. In turn, new domestic economic and political relationships spill over to the international system. Here I shall note only the essential structure of each school. The heart of the collective goods approach rests on distinctions between classes of goods, on the one hand, and economies and diseconomies of scale flowing from organizations (institutions) that deliver these goods to publics of differential size and scope, on the other.

Collective Goods Theory

Goods are whatever we want, from material things to social-psychological needs. Economists, following Samuelson, distinguish between public and private goods. Private goods are, by virtue of their production, divisible. If the producer and consumer agree on the price of a consumable good, such as a bicycle, presumably both are satisfied. The producer gets money and the consumer gets to consume the goods; there is no confusion here about who is to pay what proportion of the costs or to whom the benefits are to accrue. Public goods are analytically at the other pole of the continuum of goods. By dint of the joint nature of their consumption, goods such as national defense, law and order, and fire protection are deemed to be nonexcludable; if produced for one member of some community, these goods may not be denied to any member of that community. Of course, with public goods comes the "free rider" problem, for in the absence of the threat of sanctions, individuals have only public-spiritedness to lead them to pay.

Between public and private goods there is confusion and grist for the collective goods thesis. These goods, sometimes termed "mixed" or "collective" in nature, have externalities (spillover effects) attached to them. If, for example, I live next to a bread-making factory, I may be forced to consume the externality of the smell, the aroma produced by the bread-making process. I like the smell of bread baking and would regard this as a positive externality. No one minds being forced to consume positive externalities. However, I am forced to consume the noise pollution produced by the machinery in the plant; this is a negative externality that people do, in fact, mind being forced to consume.

Now, I use the concept of collective goods to refer to goods that are recognized as having externalities attached to them. "Pure" private goods presumably cause little public debate because these goods are excludable and divisible. Production of national defense by government receives little argument by citizens. What I am suggesting, however, is that the powerful distinction, developed by Samuelson (1954), begins to lose utility in a postindustrial world of interdependence which brings "crowding effects" with it. I will return to these distinctions, but first I need to review the economies and diseconomies of scale notion. Most sociological theories of organizations and institutions assume that larger organizations produce greater efficiency of performance, in terms of both quality and cost. Fragmentation is bad; centralization is good.

From the literatures that depart from the assumption of the individual as a being of rational choice, come very different inferences concerning the relationships between the size of an organization and economies and diseconomies of scale. It is important to distinguish between production and consumption of goods. The analysis of the internal structure of organizations on the production side comes from economic theories of organization. The consumption-side discussions derive from the collective goods literature. On the consumption side, the question is what size unit (that is, group or collective public) is most appropriate to consume what kinds of goods? While the appropriate unit for the consumption of a good such as national defense is a national unit, a neighborhood might well be a more appropriate unit upon which to base the consumption of fire and police protection (see Ostrom et al., 1973).

On the production side, the major question concerns how institutional arrangements affect the performance level of efficiency—of the institution. If a good being produced is capital-intensive, a large initial investment is spread over the quantity of output. It is in the production of such goods that familiar economies of scale accrue; that is, the greater the size of the organization, the greater the level of efficiency. However, there are a great many goods for which one encounters significant information distortion or bias and loss of control in larger compared to smaller production units. Goods that are information-sensitive (requiring many sender-receiver interactions), such as human services, are typically better served by smaller rather than larger production units (Buchanan, 1965; Williamson, 1975; Ostrom and Ostrom, 1978). Economic theorists of organizations are thus led to assume that the greater the number of vertical channels information must pass through, the greater the possibility for information distortion. For many goods, diseconomies rather than economies of scale result from the centralization of tasks.

The fundamental point is straightforward. Surely we need to think more carefully about which goods should be delivered to which publics by which size governmental organization. If one is thinking about the production of national defense, it may most efficiently be produced by a large, centralized production unit for an equally large consumption unit, the nation. However, for the same large, national consumption unit, smaller state governments might be more appropriate to produce the interstate highway network.

Many collective goods are not well served by large, centralized institutions. If my argument, presented below, that collective goods are coming to dominate the public agenda in postindustrial societies, has merit, the largely centralized institutions developed in earlier periods of social-economic change become obsolete.

Why are the number of publicly provided collective goods—about which conflict is inevitable—rising? There are at least four sets of reasons. First, as social-economic development continues, citizens apparently become more aware of the negative externalities they are forced to consume. Previously, they were willing to internalize the externalities of cigarette smoke, noise, and air pollution from public as well as private economic sources. Now they are not. The list of goods considered collective in nature grows. Second, citizens and public bureaucrats, in an unspoken conspiracy, demand that government itself provide more collective goods. For their part, citizens not only want the handicapped to be provided for; they want special transportation or educational provisions delivered. Having developed the basic social services, bureaucrats—for reasons of inter- and intraorganization competition for budgets—search for new areas of application in the public sector.

Third, public provision of goods previously provided for in the private sector, and thought to be private goods, tends to drive out remaining private provision of the goods. For example, public provision of higher education leads to a decline in the public's willingness to support private institutions of higher learning. Fourth, recall the point about interdependence being associated with postindustrial society. There may well be many positive points about increased interdependence, but the point for us is the rise in the possibility of negative externalities attached to such interdependence.

The structural change in the economy of postindustrial societies is directly related to a rise in collective goods. In turn, the rise of collective goods presents a fundamental challenge to the "normal" channels of politics. Political parties and extant governmental institutions were developed in an earlier period; new political-economic questions render their legitimacy suspect. However, there is one more theory source that questions the legitimacy of existing political and economic arrangement, the critical theory school.

Critical Theory in Postindustrial Societies

Critical theorists depart from the standard Marxist critique of social and economic change in capitalist societies to discuss whether or not systemwide transformation is apt to take place in, again, our postindustrial societies. From Marxism itself comes the argument that capitalism is a historical epoch, part of the process of historical evolution. Arguing from the perspective of the society, critical theorists look for symptoms of the breakdown of integration in economic and political systems. Of course, members of this school are hostile to capitalism and criticize the domination of the working class by the bourgeoisie. Like Marxists of the previous eras, they see the activities of capitalism, especially in the international system, as imperialism which flourishes off Third World states.

Always thinking in historical terms, critical theorists see the particular form of control (domination), definition of property rights, conceptualization of the economy, the state, and the relationship between the two as being tied to specific historical periods. They recognize the productive powers of capitalism, but feel, with postindustrial theorists, that economic change is rendering the productive sector of the economy obsolete. Unlike many postindustrial and collective goods theorists, they do not view the state as either a neutral umpire or a nuisance to be reduced. Rather the state is viewed as an essential element of the system of domination in society. The state may be much more than the expression of the interests of the dominant economic groups. The state may form a new "middle strata" that seeks to maintain itself through a variety of legitimation modes. More crucial, perhaps, are the limits of individual choice, centered by understandings attached to property, authority, and leadership.

The second contribution of critical theory may be encompassed under the concept of hegemony. Through understandings attached to what constitutes proper authority, leadership, and decision-making arrangements, the dominant classes in society maintain their positions of power. In Gramsci's evocation of hegemony, the customs, norms, and even values of a society underwrite the particular mosaic of class relationship extant in any society. Language systems become modes of domination as well, because of tacit meanings governing relationships between words. For example, authority and leadership are, in capitalist societies, understood to mean hierarchial systems of relationships between individuals and groups who are placed in asymmetrical arrangements with each other. The point is that in societies in other historical epochs, the understandings, the vocabulary describing authority, and leadership are quite different. The Gramscian contribution is to "liberate" and broaden the cultural and political dimensions of society from their status as epiphenomena strictly determined by the economic model of production under orthodox Marxism. Now, in addition to sweeping historical critiques of modern capitalism, critical theorists look for disjunctures between particular macroinstitutionalized systems of domination and individuals and interest groups governed by them. For example, Offe points to the emergence of disjunctures between authority systems at the macrosocietal level and microindividual and group levels in advanced capitalist societies. In other words, while the largely hierarchial social-economic and political institutions of society remain in place, very different types of authority are developing at the micro level—for example, on the workshop floor itself, in factories. Workers, in fact, are increasingly unwilling to put up with hierarchial authority systems and the related absence of control over their destinies.

THE NEW LIMITS OF
COMPARATIVE POLITICS

Just as the new Olson argument and the product-cycle (and comparative advantage) schools stimulate fresh thinking about what constrains economies, the recent efforts of writers I have grouped under postindustrialization, collective goods, and critical theory suggest additional inferences for politics, economics, and the relationship between the two across domestic and international boundaries. From the perspective of collective goods and critical theory, the meaning of the crisis of the state becomes clearer. "Overload" on existing political institutions is rising, as the neoconservatives lament. However, it is not warranted to assume a decline in political demands on government from citizens and interest groups. Political demands, political conflict, and "nonnormal" political participation such as neighborhood action groups, strikes, and litigation are likely to increase because of the growth in negative externalities (crowding effects of interdependence) and the inability of largely centralized social and political institutions to serve as effective conflict-resolution avenues any longer. Micro- and macro-level disjunctures between hierarchial institutions that emphasize order and individuals whose primary value increasingly becomes participation are cited by critical theorists. Moreover, earlier I cited evidence that the rise of the public sector, decline of the industrial sector, and economic growth slowdown also are features of postindustrial society. This situation may well create conditions that result in public-sector limits being reached; this, in turn, would stimulate an even greater rise in political conflict—in politics itself. (Recall, I have consciously left the effects of the energy crisis out, but it can only exacerbate the political as well as economic crisis.) Postindustrial society is the age of participation over authority, conflict over order; in short, it is the age of politics.

INFERENCES

What does this survey tell us? A basic structural transformation of one group of societies "beyond development" into postindustrial status brings with it the necessity for substantial reconceptualization of the relationships between economics and politics, between domestic and international politics. I shall note a series of tentative points.

(1) If Olson's thesis has merit, that is, if economic growth slowdown accompanies economic change in his pluralist (my postindustrial) societies, the question of equity and distribution looms large; these are political questions.

(2) If changing comparative advantage (and the product cycle) in many industries, from postindustrial to industrial countries, results in an even faster decline of the manufacturing sector, surely this must be more squarely addressed in national economic policymaking. In fact, it is difficult to believe that the law of comparative advantage will be allowed to govern. This is so because citizens in postindustrial societies are unlikely to give up easily their lifestyle expectations, their social welfare floor provided by government, or their focus on quality-of-life issues. Unlike the case of the decline of the American textile industry, in the instance of the auto and steel industries, one is talking about the potential loss of millions of jobs as a function of foreign competition. Here, then, politics dominates over standard economics.

(3) A central question, based on Olson's argument, is whether the societies that are experiencing economic growth slowdown will be able to support a tax base sufficient to support the large public sector in place in these same societies. A central question from the collective goods/postindustrial literature is whether citizens will give up the public sector.

(4) Will citizens in postindustrial societies cease their attack on the centralized nature of their institutions—societywide, so as to give their economic sector a chance to "reindustrialize"? One cannot be optimistic from the collective goods and critical theory perspectives.

(5) If we assume inferences 3 and 4, what about the domestic/international system distinctions usually drawn in and between politics and economics? Surely it is time to address explicitly the "exogenous" effects of the international system. Equally, for those who concentrate on comparative and international politics and economics, surely the devastating domestic political effects of the "rolling adjustment" of industry from postindustrial to industrial states must be considered more directly?

In sum, from somewhat distinct literatures one reaches the conclusion that it is not business as usual in postindustrial societies. For a variety of reasons the public sector has reached unprecedented heights in these societies. There are calls for dismantling the state, but citizens are unlikely to give up easily many goods and services provided by the government. They are not only resorting to collective action in more instances than before; they are also demanding an effective share of control. The demand for participation is likely to rise, not decline. Quite apart from these issues, which are largely internal to postindustrial societies, the effects of the product cycle, changing comparative advantage, and the interest-group behavior combine to produce new international system constraints on domestic economic and political behavior. We must begin to deal with these constraints directly. For example, simple "maps" of changing industrial geography patterns developed in regional international systems would be a start. Such maps would suggest international political-economy decision-making areas where common-fate situations exist. Moreover, we need to understand that the domestic political-economy realities of postindustrial societies are beginning to alter the concept of free trade with good reasons. We are just at the beginning of the cycle of efforts by domestic elites, in postindustrial societies, to raise tariff barriers. In short, we are at the beginning of new efforts to redefine both the relationships between politics and economics and the areas within which they are thought to operate.

SUMMARY

It is necessarily the case that the above sketches of the two contexts and the theory sources that appear promising are based on individualistic interpretations of recent change. Such interpretations are idiosyncratic and liable to error. Yet if one or more successful research programs are generated out of intellectual reflection of the sort represented here, the proof will be in the work of the next decade or so.

Social science is a historical enterprise and an applied subject. Yet, unlike historians, social scientists attempt to explain the present and project or even predict the future. This is as important an exercise as it is difficult. The rapidity of social change requires anticipatory designs if humans are to continue to have a hand in shaping their futures. These designs are perhaps best viewed as social architecture. All such designs are composed of three parts. First, no design will be useful if it is not linked to a reasonable description of the "real" world. Second, no design will be useful unless it grasps the most important emergent properties of the phenomena with which it is working. That is, in order to be useful, in the future, the design must have within it the sort of structuring principle that anchored the work of earlier architects such as Marx, Weber, and Keynes. Finally, the designs of major import are indeed the ones based on an explicit moral vision of the way things should be. What separates the work of our major architects of the past from the present-day futurists is the strength with which the three parts of the anticipatory designs are linked.

The continual need to develop, question, and reformulate theory (the general structuring principles that allow a temporary but necessary ordering of the political and social processes) should now be considered the most important element of the logic of inquiry on which to concentrate. If one grants this point, then the context, assumptions, conceptualization, and reconceptualization of the way the questions are formulated takes on crucial significance. This does not mean method and technique are unimportant. Breakthroughs in new methods and techniques may be required before new research programs yield productive results. "Science" is important; "history" is important.

APPENDIX

One technical point on the forms of comparison. If the *comparative* method is really not distinctive, what may be said about the three forms of comparison: cross-sectional, cross-time, and cross-level? While there has been a rekindling of interest in cross-time (longitudinal) comparison, the claims that this form of comparison is technically superior to the other two forms are invalid. In fact, what reason is there to think that urban centers in the United States in the mid-nineteenth century are equivalent to the cities of today? For some purposes they may be similar, but for other purposes they may be so different as to be different in kind from one another.

Studies using the form of cross-time comparison are subject to precisely the same criticism directed at cross-sectional studies. Cross-level comparison again is subject to the same comments made about the other two forms of comparison. Each form is useful—sometimes in combination—depending on the choice of strategy followed by the investigator. Cross-sectional comparison is used for many questions where the investigator may assume a stable universe. The benefits of cross-level analysis remain largely unexplored because of vexing level of analysis problems, but the form is potentially useful to the applicability of generalizations from larger to smaller units or the reverse. Cross-time research appears to handle some of the contextual variation problems associated with cross-sectional research.

Through the 1960s and into the 1970s, those working in quantitative comparative politics concentrated on a variety of change and stability questions, using mainly ecological and survey data. Most scholars assumed a linear relationship between standard measures of economic development, such as urbanization, industrialization, literacy, and communications and political development (however measured). It did not occur to many of us, for example, that there were upper limits on many of these measures, or that some relationships might become curvilinear or, perhaps, even inverse when studied across time. Deutsch's call in 1963 was that we were theory-rich and data-poor, and we had to rectify this situation.

As we moved into the 1970s, however, political changes of sufficient magnitude began to suggest that maybe we should reverse Deutsch's call. As we move into the 1980s, we are confused as to the merits and demerits of concepts like advanced industrial society, postindustrial society, and advanced capitalism. Leaving aside the label problem, it is increasingly apparent that several Western European societies, Canada, the United States, and Japan are moving beyond "development" into something else. We appear to be in one of these system-threshold transformations.

Scholars of all political persuasions agree, for example, that there is (1) a "crisis of the state," (2) a rapidly developing decline of parties, and (3) rapid growth of civic-action interest groups. In fact, one clue that we are in one of these system-threshold-change phases is the level of disagreement about the nature of the social-economic and political change occurring and what should be done to respond to that change. Some wish simply to damp down the increase in nonvoting-related political participation and political demands in order to save the largely centralized political institutions constructed during the industrialization phase of change. Others wish to decentralize governmental institutions. The point is that in times of flux and significant change, one sees a return to theoretical issues, to the question of the question. What are the design principles that are used to understand the world in which we live?

Our current historical situation is reminiscent of the late nineteenth and early twentieth centuries, when social scientists consciously attempted to engage in design activities because they grasped the emergent properties of the evolving industrial society. Marx, of course, was prescient about the effects of industrialization. Weber's rational theory of bureaucracy stood up well for 75 years. Keynes, Mannheim, and Laski are three figures in the early part of this century who were explicit about the threshold nature of social-economic and political change they saw occurring, and which they felt provided design opportunities in economics, the construction of the welfare state, and centralized political executive.

Recently, social and political scientists have become more historical. Scholars look back at the design of the republic,

Albert Hirschman (1977) looks at the historical process of the construction of capitalism itself, and one sees a concerted interest in critical theory from Europe. Much of critical theory boils down to efforts to grapple with larger forces of historical change that are thought to make existing institutional practices obsolete. Suddenly, we have many new propositions and ideas to check out.

I have avoided discussing, in detail, quantitative historical work. I wish only to assert here that I believe a good deal of comparative research that uses cross-time data violates the requirements of the process assumption I alluded to earlier. To wrench data out of its historical context in order to construct multiple variable sets across time on alliance systems, participation, or conflict creates concept-equivalence problems in the same way that many cross-sectional studies do. What is my answer? I think we should engage a great deal more in what might be called contextual modeling of significant social and political processes across time.

Earlier I noted the concept pluralism. The content of the concept of pluralism should be understood now as arising out of a particular historical context. I think that the mainstream of American political science is still guided by this pluralist vision of politics. For example, under the pluralist conceptualization, the state is viewed as distinct from the economy and as simply the sum of distinctive aggregations. These distinctive aggregations include Congress, the political parties, and individual and collective elements of local, regional, and national bureaucratic interests.

From several points of view, this view of the state appears dated. Elsewhere, with Raymond Duvall (1980), I have attempted to distinguish four models of the state arrayed in ascending complexity. The pluralist vision noted here falls under, and captures, the first and simplest model of the state. The other models of the state include the state as administrative order, the state as legal order, and the state as embodied in language and culture. The way we should conceptualize the role of the state in economy and society is, of course, debatable.

However, it does appear, as we move into the 1980s, that the pluralist model of the state is dated, naive, and only of historical interest. Again, how one should view state/economy relationships is an important question. Is the state best seen as a captive of economic interests (Lindbloom, 1977), or is the economy increasingly dominated by the state? I do not believe my assessment of pluralism is quite so debatable. The pluralist vision of politics was developed out of the particular historical experience of the United States, and I think the best American work of political science in the pluralist tradition of the 1950s and 1960s is interpretable in this light.

NOTES

1. By "postindustrial" I mean the point at which the service, especially including the public sector, accounts for a greater proportion of the economy than the industrial sector. In societies such as Great Britain, Denmark, Sweden, and Holland, the public sector itself accounts for approximately one-half of the gross national product. For the United States and Canada the size of the public sector is moving fairly close to the British case. See my *The Limits of Politics: Collective Goods and Political Change in Postindustrial Societies* (1980) for further discussion of the distinction.

2. By which, again, I shall mean simply the point where the greatest proportion of the economic activity comes to be generated in the public as compared to the market sector of the economy. The literature on late capitalism deals with societies in this situation (see Offe, 1975; O'Conner, 1973; Miliband, 1969; Wright, 1978).

REFERENCES

Almond, G. A. and G. B. Powell, Jr. (1966) *Comparative Politics: A Developmental Approach.* Boston: Little, Brown.
Baumol, W. J. (1967) "Macroeconomics of unbalanced growth: the anatomy of urban crisis." *American Economic Review* 57 (June): 415-426.
Bell, D. (1973) *The Coming of Post-Industrial Society.* New York: Basic Books.
Benjamin, R. (1980) *The Limits of Politics: Collective Goods and Political Change in Postindustrial Societies.* Chicago: University of Chicago Press.
——— and R. Duvall (1980) "The role of the state in post-colonial and post-industrial capitalist societies." Presented at the American Political Science Association meetings, Washington, D.C., September.
Brunner, R. D. and K. Liepelt (1972) "Data analysis, process analysis, and system change." *Midwest Journal of Political Science* 16, 4: 538-569.

Buchanan, J. (1965) "An economic theory of clubs." *Economica* 32 (February): 1-15.

Cortes, F., A. Przeworski, and J. Sprague (1974) *Systems Analysis for Social Scientists.* New York: John Wiley.

Dahl, R. (1961) *Who Governs?* New Haven, CT: Yale University Press.

Deutsch, K. (1963) *The Nerves of Government.* New York: Free Press.

Habermas, J. (1973) *Legitimation Crisis.* Boston: Beacon Press.

Hirschman, A. D. (1977) *The Passions and the Interests.* Princeton, NJ: Princeton University Press.

Huntington, S. (1968) *Political Order in Changing Societies.* New Haven, CT: Yale University Press.

Inglehart, R. (1977) *The Silent Revolution.* Princeton, NJ: Princeton University Press.

Kurth, J. (1979) "The political consequences of the product cycle: industrial history and political outcomes." *International Organization* 33, 1: 1-34.

Lakatos, I. (1970) "Falsification and the methodology of scientific research programmes," pp. 71-196 in I. Lakatos and A. Musgrave (eds.) *Criticism and the Growth of Knowledge.* Cambridge, MA: Harvard University Press, 71-196.

Lindbloom, C. (1977) *Politics and Markets.* New York: Basic Books.

Lipset, S. (1960) *Political Man.* Garden City, NY: Doubleday.

Lowi, T. (1979) *The End of Liberalism.* New York: Norton.

Miliband, R. (1969) *The State in Capitalist Society.* London: Weidenfeld & Nicolson.

O'Conner, J. (1973) *The Fiscal Crisis of the State.* New York: St. Martin's Press.

Offe, C. (1975) *Wohlfahrtsstaat und Massenloyalität.* Köln: Kiepenhaver & Witsch.

Olson, M. (forthcoming) *The Political Economy of Comparative Economic Growth in Pluralistic Societies.* New Haven, CT: Yale University Press.

Olson, M. (1965) *The Logic of Collective Action.* Cambridge, MA: Harvard University Press.

Ostrom, E., R. B. Parks, and G. P. Whitaker (1973) "Do we really want to consolidate urban police forces? a reappraisal of some old assertions." *Public Administration Review* 33 (September/October): 423-433.

Ostrom, V. and E. Ostrom (1978) "Public goods and public choices," pp. 7-49 in E. S. Savas (ed.) *Alternatives for Delivering Public Services: Toward Improved Performance.* Boulder, CO: Westview.

Przeworski, A. and H. Teune (1970) *The Logic of Comparative Social Inquiry.* New York: John Wiley.

Samuelson, P. (1954) "The pure theory of public expenditure." *Review of Economic Statistics* (November): 386-389.

Williamson, O. (1975) *Markets and Hierarchies: Analysis and Antitrust Implications.* New York: Free Press.

Wright, E. O. (1978) *Class, Crisis and State.* London: NLB.

4

Is There a Micro Theory Consistent with Contextual Analysis?

JOHN SPRAGUE

The term "contextual effect" describes variation in political behavior that depends, systematically, on properties of the environment within which that behavior is embedded. The crucial substantive issue for contextual theories turns on the degree of independence obtaining between what my neighbors do and who they are, and what I do. Reasoning, which takes as its starting point the interdependence of human behavior, leads in a natural way to forms of theory and strategies of analysis having an emphatically sociological flavor. One form in which that flavor manifests itself is work that falls under the broad rubric of contextual analysis or contextual effects. This essay falls in the sociological, not the economic, reasoning tradition. It seeks to detail the logic by which a set of relatively explicit individual-level hypotheses lead to contextual effects on political behavior, that is, to dependence of individual political behavior on variation in properties in the individual's environment.

AUTHOR'S NOTE: The work presented here is based on joint work with Professor Louis P. Westefield of Southern Illinois University, Edwardsville. He is not responsible for my errors in analysis, interpretation, or judgment. Without the collaboration we have enjoyed, however, there would be no chapter here. In particular, the theory developed in the last section is taken from a joint paper with him (1979a). This work

Issues of method frequently dominate discussions of the effects of environmental context on behavior, but these will be mostly set aside in the discussion that follows. I assume at the outset that contextual effects on political behavior are substantial and that ignoring them, or, more usually, denying them, assures substantial misunderstanding in our knowledge of political behavior. The identification of a systematic association between variation in behavior and variation in environmental properties goes back at least to the publication of Emile Durkheim's *Suicide* at the turn of the century and finds its first modern statement in research in political behavior in the writing of Herbert Tingsten (1937). Political scientists have exhibited a renewed interest in contextual analysis, which leads me to hope that·revisions of an overindividualized view of political behavior may be on the way.

WHAT IS CONTEXTUAL ANALYSIS?

A contextual theory specifies the individual and environmental properties, and also the environmental unit or scope of aggregation, that determine variation in a given behavior of interest. Theory also specifies the *form* of the dependency. A minimal bit of notation is convenient for fixing ideas. Let y_{ij} measure the behavior for the ith individual in the jth context where the contextual units indexed by j are of a scope of aggregation that is dictated by the theory. Similarly, in the simplest case, which is paradigmatic and all that is needed, let x_{ij} represent a theoretically chosen individual property for the

was supported in part by National Science Foundation Grant SOC-77-19938 to Washington University. The survey employed in the analyses was supplied through the Inter-University Consortium for Political and Social Research, located in the Center for Political Studies of the Institute for Social Research, University of Michigan. Professor Westefield and I are grateful for timely assistance from Professor Warren Miller, Ms. Ann Robinson, and Maria Sanchez. The original principal investigators are in no way responsible for my use of their data. A small army of graduate students has worked on this project over the past three to four years. I wish to note the cheerful and efficient contributions of Mike Wolfe, Cathy Gurganus, Rob McDonald, Chris Johnsen, Courtney Brown, and Greg Weiher.

i^{th} individual in the jth context and let z_{ij} represent a measure on the environment of the ith individual in the jth context; that is, z_{ij} is based on the jth environment. Hence a contextual theory may be characterized informally by

$$y_{ij} = f(x_{ij}, z_{ij}) \qquad\qquad [1]$$

where x and z are, perhaps, vectors of individual and environmental observables, and f is a theoretically dictated functional form.

Just how deterministic or stochastic one wishes to make equation 1 is an important matter for theory and application but not critical for our purposes here. However, equation 1 is precise enough to characterize sharply the two most important substantive strategies considered in contextual analysis and to illustrate the property that makes a theory contextual. A theory is contextual when variation in z_{ij} produces variation in y_{ij}. In a formal sense, deductions to the behavior y include predicates which take z as nontrivial arguments, that is, which rely on z to obtain the required deductions. Hence, a measure beyond the individual is formally necessary to an explanation that appeals in part to contextual hypotheses. The substantive strategies require elaboration.

Restrict equation 1 to the simplest possible case, where x and z are single observables. The most common strategy of contextual analysis is to consider a case where z is some composition, typically a mean, of x in the jth context. This hypothesis can be termed "social resonance," since the underlying intuition is one of reinforcement of a property possessed by the individual through repeatedly encountering the same property in the environment. It may be written as

$$y_{ij} = f(x_{ij}, z_{ij} = \bar{x}._{j}) \text{ (social resonance)} \qquad\qquad [2]$$

where

$$\bar{x}._{j} = (1/(n_j - 1)) \sum_{k} x_{kj} \text{ for } k \neq i \text{ and}$$

n_j = number of individuals in the jth context

Thus z_{ij} is a composition over all members of the jth context except individual i. In practice the mean of some conveniently available aggregate unit is used, since the effect of the ith individual's score will be negligible in the contextual units typically available. This procedure has led to a truly vast methodological literature in sociology focused on school effects in the sociological analysis of educational achievement, aspiration, advantages, and so on.

In political science the classic empirical statement of the model of equation 2 is in an early paper by Warren Miller (1956). In that paper, Miller showed that the rate at which a Democratic propensity (x_{ij}) was translated into behavior (y_{ij}) was also dependent in an interactive fashion on the distribution of other Democratic propensities ($\bar{x}_{.j}$) in the individual's environment. Democrats living in areas of high Democratic density were more likely to vote for the Democratic presidential candidate than Democrats of the same measured level of motivation who lived surrounded by Republicans. This study remains one of the few attempts to demonstrate contextual effects with national samples and fits nicely to the structure sketched by equation 2.

The structure of equation 2 also provides a picture of the finding by Butler and Stokes (1969: 144-150) in Great Britain, that upper-class persons increased their rate of conservative-party support as the constituencies in which they lived became more heavily upper-class. They report a similar effect for working-class citizens and Labour party support. A third example from Great Britain comes from W. L. Miller (1978) and is consistent with the Butler and Stokes results from an earlier period. The form of reasoning illustrated by equation 2 is relatively common in contextual analyses.

Matching the notion of social resonance in a formal sense is the hypothesis of behavioral contagion, which is found much less frequently in the literature. In this case z is some composition of y. This may be written as

$$y_{ij} = f(x_{ij}, z_{ij} = \bar{y}_{.j}) \text{ (behavioral contagion)} \qquad [3]$$

where

$$\bar{y}_{\cdot j} = (1/(n_j - 1))\sum_k y_{kj} \text{ for } k \neq i \text{ and}$$

n_j = number of individuals in the jth context

Whereas in the case of equation 2, assuming a linear form for f can ultimately lead to a reasonable statistical unraveling of individual and social resonance effects (Alwin, 1976; Boyd and Iversen, 1979), the same simple hypothesis leads to complex statistical problems for the model of equation 3. As far as I know, this substantive argument and an attempt to model it were first put forth by Isambert (1960) for the curious phenomenon of civil burials in Paris. Boudon has considered this problem (1963; 1967; discussed by Sprague and Westefield, 1979b) for aggregate data analysis. A complex treatment of the statistical issues is contained in Erbring and Young (1979). Erbring and Young make clear that an inherent dynamic component in the notion of behavioral contagion is difficult to treat from a static perspective. The methodological difficulty is easily visualized as a sampling problem. If I sample voters in Duchess County and discover 40 percent vote for the Democratic party, how can I sort out those who vote for the Democratic party because their neighbors do? All models of this problem of which I am aware lead to complex and nonlinear formulations.

Two final remarks on the coerciveness of scientific procedure are in order. Contextual analyses of mass political behavior with American national probability samples number at most a half-dozen studies. Yet a much larger number of studies emphasizing the importance of context are available at the level of communities or small regions (Stockholm, Santiago, Columbus, Buffalo, Scotland, Wales). The reason probably lies in the logic of the probability sample. To obtain, for instance, a sample that is representative of the American electorate, one proceeds to pluck individuals out of the contexts in which they live and work. This makes contextual analysis particularly difficult, for the context is almost never measured in national samples. On the other hand, scientists working in restricted areas or cities, probably where they live themselves, are sensitive to the variation in environments. It is part of their local common knowledge, and they make special efforts to secure measures of environmental properties.

The second methodological remark turns on habits of scientific thought that also arise from sampling procedures. The sample survey measures variables by securing individual self-reports. This leads, occasionally, to the presumption that survey measurements are individual as opposed to contextual or social. Yet some common individual measures (say, occupation or education) are obvious proxies for a complex individual history, and index theoretically relevant, current social embedding. This should not be confused with the methodologically bad habit of calling unexplained, between-aggregate unit variance a contextual effect, which Hauser (1970a, 1970b) has correctly and repeatedly criticized. Rather, I wish to emphasize that many observations we commonly treat as individual properties acquire theoretical power precisely because they are proxy measures for a rich contextual experience. Unless one proceeds like an economist and assumes that people just have their preferences—that preferences are not fit subjects for scientific explanation—one should, on reflection, recognize that many of the common individual-level measures used in research on political behavior appear as precipitates of the contexts within which they were acquired. It does no harm to use the measured property, say an attitude, directly in research, but it is perhaps too easy to lose sight of the behavioral origin of the attitude.

It is one thing to demonstrate a contextual effect, even, let us suppose, in a methodologically flawless fashion. It is quite another matter to show *why* the effect is reasonable. How does the observed covariation between environmental property and individual behavior arise? What is the behavioral mechanism producing the contextual effect? What theory can be offered that leads us to expect such patterns? These questions are taken up in two stages. First, the principal mechanisms commonly adduced to account for contextual effects are sketched. Second, an explicit informal theory is set out which develops one of the mechanisms in detail in an attempt to provide a fairly complete micropremise underpinning for the observed macro-level covariation. However, before we turn to those tasks, an empirical example is in order.

AN EMPIRICAL EXAMPLE OF A CONTEXTUAL EFFECT

The purpose of this example is to show that quite elementary models can be empirically complex and pose interesting interpretive problems. The results are taken from a longer report (Sprague, 1981) and are based on analyses of the 1976 national election study of the Center for Political Studies, University of Michigan.

The criterion behavior examined is the distribution of partisan identification, which is conventionally scored on a seven-point scale running from 0 (strong Democrat) through 6 (strong Republican). Partisan identification is studied here by means of the general linear model estimated by ordinary least squares. The model employed has been systematically justified by Alwin (1976) for the simplest case and extended to include interaction by Boyd and Iversen (1979). It is well known that partisan identification contains a large component of variation that arises from socialization in the home. Party identification is inherited. It is also suspected that conditions at entry to adult political experience may permanently affect this distribution. These two sources of variation are entered as controls by sorting the population for the party identification of the respondent's father and by explicitly including the respondent's age as a regressor.

The classic status variable of education is taken as the independent observation measured in years at the individual and tract levels. There are three questions of interest: (1) Does respondent's education structure the distribution of partisanship? (2) Does the distribution of education among respondent's neighbors (the environment or context) structure the distribution of partisanship? (3) Is there cross-level (indi-

TABLE 4.1   Slopes of Partisan Identification on Respondent's Education
(I), Mean Tract Education (T), and Cross-Level Education
Interaction (I^*T), Controlling for Respondent's Age in
Father Republican Condition for 1976 Within-Tract Sample

	Value	T-Test Prob Value
Constant	−15.837	.0003
	(4.279)*	
Education		
I	+ 1.280	.0001
	(.314)	
T	+ 1.662	.0001
	(.386)	
I^*T	− 0.113	.0001
	(.028)	
Age	+ 0.0214	.0003
	(.0059)	
R^2	.083	
N	326	

*Standard errors in parentheses.

vidual with contextual) interaction? These questions are investigated in the presence of controls for father's party and respondent's age. Under some conditions, all three questions can be
answered yes. The regression results are exhibited in Table 4.1
for respondents with Republican fathers. The effects of education are displayed in Figure 4.1 in a three-dimensional plot that
vividly portrays the interaction between individual and contextual education on partisanship as a twisted plane in that space.
The point of view of the observer for Figure 4.1 is upward, to
the right, and back away from the plane of the page.

The sample is truncated in two important ways. First, the
analysis is based only on those respondents who live in census
tracts. Second, only those who report having Republican fathers
are included. Thus, context is taken to be the neighborhood and
is proxied by the educational mean of the census tract in which
the respondent resides, measured by the census report of the

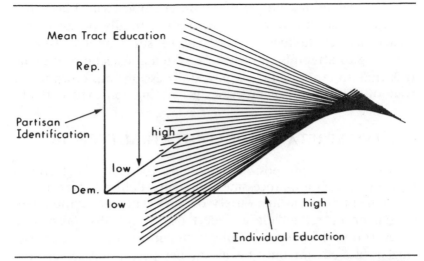

Figure 4.1 Three-Dimensional Projection of Interaction Effect Between Respondent's Education and Respondent's Census Tract Mean Education on Partisan Identification for the 1976 Within-Tract Sample in the Republican Father Condition

mean and weighted in the analysis by respondent frequency. Table 4.1 shows that the results are statistically crisp. The contextual effect for education is of the same order of magnitude as the individual-level effect (indeed, it has a larger slope). Significant statistical interaction is found between contextual-level and individual-level education. The presence of a measure of education at the individual level does not remove or control the effect of education as a contextual measure at the level of aggregation of the census tract.

The geometry of the interaction between levels of observation of education displayed in Figure 4.1 hints at the complexity of the explanatory task that ultimately must be faced by the theorist who appeals to contextual argument. The theory fragment developed in the last section of this chapter attempts to speak only to the coefficient on tract education, that is, to account for its sign and why that coefficient is nonzero relative to the individual level coefficient. The theory fragment leaves for another place and another theoretical attempt explanations for the sign and magnitude of the interaction term. I hope this example illustrates to, even if it does not totally persuade, the reader that contextual effects may be substantial and hence deserving of attempts to provide a systematic account of them. It is time to abandon this empirical digression and return to the issue of mechanisms or processes generating contextual effects.

INTERPRETATION OF CONTEXTUAL EFFECTS

Most mechanisms posited as sources for contextual effects turn on information-processing arguments. Political information is supplied to citizens in a variety of ways. The information may be salient or redundant and certainly frequently noisy and hence (often deliberately) ambiguous. Information reaches the citizen filtered not only by his or her perceptual screen—the reception bias of the individual—but also by the personally immediate social system within which the individual lives and works. One may ignore coworkers and neighbors, of course, but this may be no less consequential than interacting with them. Consequences for individual political behavior arise from the embedding of the individual in such microenvironments— environments that are likely to be both informationally biased and interpersonally reactive. It is in these politically nonneutral and interactive contexts that political information is received, nurtured, matured, and ultimately brought to bear on individual acts of political participation, public-policy support, and partisanship.

The basic distinction among mechanisms of contextual influence is between specifying a structure for the action system, the dynamics, of the process of informationally relevant social interaction, on the one hand, and positing the psychological mechanisms of individual calculation, on the other hand. The descriptive questions become: To whom do you talk? In what pattern? About what? With what consequences? The first three questions are directed to the structure of social interaction, its form, and its content, while the last goes to the laws of individual calculation that are presumed to govern the processing of the information received by the individual.

Reference-group arguments for contextual effects contain the joint themes of contexts as sources of standards from community norms and as sources of benchmarks for comparison of self with others. Motivated conformity to community norms was considered by Putnam (1966) and found wanting as an explanation for the classic findings of Warren Miller (1956) on the effects of political context. In a nonpolitical setting the comparative role of context in guiding individual judgments is well illustrated by a study of career decisions by college men (Davis, 1966) with the marvelous title, "The campus as a Frog Pond."

Somewhere between laws of comparative judgment and a full specification of the process of social interaction lies the field of social network analysis (Kadushin, 1979). In applications to political behavior, social network analysis formulates the contextual effects problem as one of specifying the circle of acquaintances with whom conversation that has political content takes place. This leads, for example, to a criticism of contextual analysis because it frequently uses the respondent's address as a means of determining relevant contexts (Eulau and Siegel, 1980). The criticism is well taken in terms of existing substantive work but poses no contradiction at the level of theory. In most formulations of contextual analysis, the theoretical appeal is to social-interaction processes (Segal and Meyer, 1974; Cox, 1969), and the social network perspective simply emphasizes that better information about the structure of social interaction should lead to more successful empirical work.

The final mechanism to be considered is the social-interaction process alone, fleshed out in greater detail in the next section. Useful discussions can be found in Coleman (1964) and Przeworski (1974), although the central formulation followed below is due to William McPhee. The typical argument runs along the lines that as social interactions become more frequent, the influence of the interactions becomes greater, especially as the informational content of those interactions becomes more homogeneous. The classic article demonstrating such effects on political behavior is by McClosky and Dahlgren (1959) and turns on an interpretation of the influence of primary groups.

Table 4.1 is also consistent with this view in one important respect. The coefficients on the individual-level and tract-level regressors carry the same sign. One might reason that this is consistent with simple reinforcement through social interaction which is within the paradigm of equation 2—social resonance. The true situation depicted in Table 4.1 and Figure 4.1 is much more complicated, of course, because of the interaction effect, but attention should be focused on this consistency in sign between individual and contextual levels in reading the theoretical development that comes next. A theory for the interaction effects must await treatment in another place at another time. What micro-based theory can be offered to account for such patterns, especially sign consistency?

THE PROCESS OF SOCIAL INTERACTION

The basic theoretical problem can be put as a question: What are the mechanisms that connect microenvironments with individual political behavior? Or, more boldly put, how does social structure coerce individual behavior?

One set of facts is worth keeping in mind. Context apparently affects all groups. In particular, high-status individuals are subject to contextual effects. Segal and Meyer (1974) show this, and Menzel and Katz (1955-1956) have shown this for a group as specialized as medical doctors with respect to a matter that lies within their presumed professional competence. This is in rather sharp contrast to the information-flow responsiveness of individuals independent of context as presented by Converse (1962) and replicated by Orbell (1970). Blau (1961) has shown that the aged do not escape contextual forces, and certainly the acquisition of a partisan identification through socialization in the home is contextual; hence the young do not escape either.

Watching the evening news, probably an atypical behavior in the mass, nevertheless may be used as a prototypical situation for behavior in a microenvironment, that is, contextually embedded behavior. Turning on the TV set is volitional. Paying attention may also be volitional, but, assuming that the information supplied by the news report commands attention, it must be processed. Both the information and the opinion supplied may be discrepant or congruent with the watcher's existing knowledge and opinions. The broadcast may produce modification in beliefs through private, within-the-individual processing of information. The broadcast may elicit an expression of opinion or a curse. This in turn may produce responses from friends or family if they in turn pay attention to the TV watcher's behavior. And so on.

Three features of this situation are fundamental. First, information is processed contingent on individual attention. Second, behavior begets the behavior of others in response contingent on the interpersonal communication of information. Third, these events occur with very high frequency relative to the rate at which they are typically sampled by social scientists. Most of the behavior that occurs in this microenvironment is measured indirectly if at all. If reference-group psychological mechanisms are central to understanding mass political behavior, it is in such contexts that some group identifications are learned and many are reinforced. If adult social learning and reinforcement through social interaction are important for understanding mass political behavior, it is in such microenvironments that selective exposure to information and interaction occurs, producing characteristic propensities to act and typical attitudes in groups similarly situated.

Politics or information from the political system plays the substantive role of providing stimuli for the individual in the form of campaign information, public officials' publicized decisions, scandal, party workers' knocks on the front door, and so forth. The individual pays attention (or not) to these stimuli and engages (or not) in expressive response. The social system in which the individual is embedded then responds (or not) to the individual's behavior. Thus, a fundamental property of the microcontext of behavior is the contingent nature of social interaction. From the perspective of systematic observation, analysis, and theory, it is inherently stochastic, if nevertheless structured and patterned.

The nature of this social-system response and the subsequent individual return response is where the heart of the effectiveness of social interaction lies. The individual will be confirmed in his or her beliefs or disconfirmed in them depending on the quality of the interaction. The consequences for change or strengthening of beliefs depend also on what further informational search the individual engages in, especially an information search prompted by incongruencies or uncertainties induced by social interaction. The individual then engages (or not) in further information search and may or may not modify his or her beliefs as a result of the joint effects of social interaction and subsequent informational search. The loop is thus closed (it is feedback) and the process repeats. But the process is continuous in time, more or less, and occurs with high frequency.

Thus we have three natural dynamics associated with the study of mass political behavior: the long-run time of periodic elections and electoral epochs; the short-run time of particular campaigns, in which most of our studies (surveys) are conducted; and the very short-run time or high frequency of behavior in the microenvironment, seldom if ever directly measured. The theoretical effort here is to flesh out more fully the structure of these high-frequency dynamics in the microenvironment.

The issue of attention may be settled for present purposes by assuming that some information is attended to with some frequency, and that some individual expressive behaviors are attended to by the individual's immediate social environment (Converse, 1962; Orbell, 1970). The crucial interaction mechanism follows work of McPhee (1963; McPhee and Smith, 1962; McPhee and Ferguson, 1962; McPhee with Smith and Ferguson, 1963) based on ideas of Kurt Lewin. McPhee's formulation is supplemented here by an elaboration of properties of social interaction interpreted in operant-conditioning terms. This is not a new idea (Homans, 1961). A readable overview of modern developments may be found in Laming (1973), but reliance is placed not on learning theory but rather on simple properties of experimental reinforcement schedules as studied before World War II, especially by Skinner.

The power of McPhee's characterization of social interaction arises from its elegant reconciliation of social influence and individual behavior. No units of social influence are transferred from one individual to another; rather, the social environment, on the occasion of a conversation about politics—a politically relevant social interaction—can only bring home to the individual that his or her own beliefs, and those of his or her friends, are not congruent. What does a sensible person then do? He reconsiders his own position in light of the fact that his close associates, whom he respects or holds affection for, or both, disagree with him. (Disagreement is the interesting case.) But reconsideration means gathering information anew and forming a new judgment on this new basis. *The process of information search is almost certainly carried out in an environment that contains pronounced informational biases—biases most probably congruent with the beliefs of associates, that is, biases typical of the microcontext of behavior, typical of social structure.* Thus the result of incongruence between objective reality (personal beliefs as modified by political information individually processed) and social reality (the beliefs of friends) is likely to be information search in an informationally structured environment leading to modification of individual beliefs. This modification probably is biased in the direction typical of the microenvironment. For purposes of the dynamics of belief modification, it does not matter whether the psychological mechanism producing modification is simply the rational acquisition of misinformation or affectively motivated modification arising from some dissonance-reduction mechanism. The important result is change in belief. Either psychological assumption, or perhaps others, will do.

The basic mechanism of social influence through social interaction assumes that social approval or disapproval is rewarding or punishing, that it constitutes some rough equivalent of positive and negative reinforcement with respect to some expressive behavior by the individual. The effect of negative reinforcement, however, is not to extinguish a learned habit but rather to cause the individual to reconsider. Positive reinforcement may be interpreted classically as contributing to habit strength. It confirms the individual in his or her beliefs and prejudices. It is reasonable to suppose this is the typical outcome of interaction in the microenvironment. The basic hypothesis is that these interactions go on regularly and frequently in the multiple microcontexts in which the individual conducts his or her day-to-day affairs.

Rapid, face-to-face interactions in a primary group provide feedback for participants with virtually no time delay. Reinforcement is known to be more efficient as the time delay between the behavior to be reinforced and the reinforcement becomes small. But this condition must be ideally realized in a primary group. Thus, members of such groups, engaged in mutual social interaction and its attendant social learning, ought to exhibit similar political behaviors (McClosky and Dahlgren, 1959). Furthermore, efficiency of learning is related to frequency of reinforcement; hence, the primary group also must be more efficient in this respect than most other social formations. It follows that properties of primary groups, such as the family or coworkers (McClosky and Dahlgren, 1959; Cox, 1974; Finifter, 1974; Merelman, 1968), are more powerful predictors of individual behavior than the neighborhood (Segal and Meyer, 1974), the census tract (Segal and Wildstrom, 1970), or the "social area" (Green, 1971).

In addition to time delay between behavior and reinforcement and frequency of reinforcement, the homogeneity of the reinforcement is important. Both McClosky and Dahlgren (1959) and Segal and Meyer (1974) show that the homogeneity of microenvironments is associated with increased predictive power. This homogeneity is another face of frequency. Homogeneity may be interpreted to mean that the multiple microenvironments of the individual are all trying to teach or encourage him or her in the same beliefs and behaviors. Indeed, when social change or mobility decrease this homogeneity of the microenvironment, substantial political consequences apparently follow (Valen and Katz, 1964).

A fourth property turns on the extent to which the analogy between social interaction and operant conditioning holds. The nature of the schedule itself—continuous or intermittent, variable or fixed—may be important. This leads to some immediate expectations concerning attitudes toward public policy and their susceptibility to contextual influences. Policy questions that arise for the first time in the context of a political campaign or are for the first time systematically thrust forward to the attention of the mass public in a political campaign should be highly dynamic and contextually dependent for two reasons. First, having been matters of idiosyncratic private opinion before, such issues do not possess a history of discussion; that is, they are not embedded in past social learning. Second, the discussion in social interaction during the campaign may approximate a continuous reinforcement schedule for such issues, producing rapid change in the distribution of such issues in the mass public structured by social context. Continuous reinforcement teaches rapidly but provides poor protection against extinction. Take away the campaign and deterioration may be anticipated. Perhaps this mechanism contributes to the instability in attitudes reported from the panel studies. Intermittent conditioning, on the other hand, produces slow learning but is resistant to extinction. The persistence of attachment to party—party identification—is consistent with a view of the political socialization process as intermittent reinforcement of the maturing child's beliefs.

Finally, the individual's motivational state is of prime importance. Learning is known to be more efficient when motivation is high. This may be interpreted here as influencing attention. Hence, when motivation is high (the issue is salient), individuals will attend to their informational environment relevant to that issue. *But this means, ceteris paribus, that expressive responses to informational stimuli are more likely and hence politically significant social interactions are likely to be more frequent.* If the issue is salient but policy stands of politicians or officials are highly ambiguous, then one might anticipate the consequences of social interaction will be maximal. This is consistent with the results of Segal and Meyer (1974) showing an interaction between political and social context. They show that when the political context is maximally ambiguous, the effects of social context are greatest. This brings us back once more to the interpretation of politics as information stimuli attended to in greater or lesser degree by the individual. The most important properties of political stimuli will be their match to individual motivational states and their ambiguity.

This informal assemblage of ideas produces a theory fragment on contextual effects from which at least some expectations may be extracted. Deductions or predictions of social context effects, political context effects, and the joint effects of both arise from variations in the individual's microenvironmental embedding and from variation in political information and organization. In applications, the problem is to produce hypotheses about the interaction-information system of the microenvironment.

Social structure enters the theory as determining probable reinforcement schedules; in other words, social structure furnishes experimental conditions realizing differing reinforcement phenomena. Social structure also provides complex filters biasing the information available in the individual's environment. Finally, social structure may determine directions of influence by biases in attention mechanisms due to status difference or affect. The latter can be thought of as fear (of the boss), respect (for parents or friends), and love (for peers, family, parents). Individual psychology enters the theory as determining attention and mechanisms of adjustment to incongruent social and objective perceptions. Politics enters as furnishing information to the individual that may or may not result in behaviors with interactive social consequences.

The stability of patterns of attitude and behavior over time, to the extent that they are contextually dependent, arises from highly dynamic contextual processes. It is precisely when social interactions are disrupted that their typically confirming and thus stabilizing properties are jeopardized. Thus, macrosocial movements such as the flight to the suburbs following World War II may have had disruptive effects on earlier patterns of behavior through the transformations brought about in social-interaction systems in microenvironments, both for movers and stayers. The most important empirical rule that emerges is the notion that contextual effects will be more powerful the closer empirical measurement approaches the theoretical unit of the primary group and the closer measurement estimates true frequencies of interaction.

This view of the process of social interaction contains some elements that may be tied to the information typically available in surveys. Other classes of desired information may be obtained with difficulty or not at all. Attention is one essential ingredient, and it is reasonable to suppose, for example, that highly educated individuals are likely to be more attentive to all kinds of information. This should also be true, in the case of a public policy, for those for whom the issue is salient, the highly motivated. The systematic bias in the individual's information environment must be correlated with environmental social structure or social embedding. Features of the social embedding may be measured in a number of ways, including use of the individual respondent's place of residence as an index to information on social structure. From another perspective, issue salience as a measure of motive is important. Not only do the highly motivated pay attention, but they also, in principle, should be more susceptible to learning from social interaction. Frequency of interaction is more difficult to get at, as is the specification of the interaction scope and the content of the interactions. One measure that might bear on these issues, however, would be the group memberships of the individual, which frequently are available. Thus, there are a number of kinds of information that may allow connecting the social-interaction process to readily available information from surveys or census sources. *Hence, the theory can be assigned empirical content.*

The particular consequences of interaction depend, according to the theory, on attention, motivation, and interaction patterns. Surrogates for these three conditions potentially affecting the efficiency of social interaction can be constructed from survey responses. Interaction patterns are, of course, difficult to reconstruct. Without specifying what the direction of influence should be or what the synergism with context might be, it is still reasonable to believe that persons who report activity in various kinds of groups are likely to have interaction patterns markedly different from those who report no such activity. Hence, interaction may be measured indirectly and inferentially by information on group memberships. Our theory is silent on the potential interactions among attention, motivation, and interaction patterns. There is no reason arising from the theory to expect one condition to control another or, alternatively, to expect them to be highly interactive or, for that matter, highly additive either.

In the view of social-interaction processes developed here, the mechanism of contextual effects arising from social interaction is complex. It is consistent with the notion of social resonance discussed in connection with equation 2. In the formulation just set out, the individual emerges as an information processor, variable in motivation and attention and information environment. The information environment is biased. A good clue to this bias may be direct measures on the social or behavioral structure of appropriate contexts. Social embedding determines not only interaction opportunities, and perhaps their probable content, but also the reinforcement schedules typical in the individual's varying interaction contexts, although this may be always beyond direct measurement. Dynamics in mass political behavior are driven by a perceived discrepancy between personal beliefs and the beliefs of significant others, not necessarily peers, in the individual's environment of social interaction. The essential condition for potential behavioral change thus is incongruence between personal belief and perception of the beliefs of others. Finally, the entire process and its behavioral consequences are highly contingent. Citizens may or may not pay attention, may or may not expostulate, may or may not provoke the response of others, and so on. This construction has an inherently stochastic flavor.

In light of this argument there is no magic in contextual effects. They arise in this formulation as the natural consequence of (1) laws of social learning, (2) the pattern of social interaction, (3) the informational content coming both to the individual and to his or her social network, and (4) biases in these processes imposed by that great experimenter social structure. The observed covariation between individual-level behavior and a measure on the individual's environment—a contextual effect—is no longer substantively problematic. The intermediary microevents that determine the macroevent have been constructed theoretically. From this perspective, the regression coefficients on education at the individual and tract contextual levels exhibited in Table 4.1 might be expected to exhibit similar signs.

SUMMARY

This essay has characterized the phrase "contextual effect" by detailing some meanings for it in the literature and by giving an elementary quantitative example. Informal paradigms of the two most discussed theoretical variants—social resonance and behavioral contagion—were offered, and the empirical example was taken to be typical of social resonance. Finally, an informal theory was presented which accounts for the agreement in sign between individual and contextual effects for the same observable measured at the two levels. The theory is based on hypotheses specifying the logic of the microprocesses that may generate contextual effects.

REFERENCES

Alwin, D. F. (1976) "Assessing school effects: some identities." *Sociology of Education* 49: 294-303.
Blau, Z. S. (1961) "Structural constraints on friendships in old age." *American Sociological Review* 26: 429-439.
Boudon, R. (1963) "Propriétés individuelles et propriétés collectives: une problème d'analyse écologique." *Review Française de Sociologie* 4: 275-299.
——— (1967) *L'Analyse Mathematique des Faits Sociaux.* Paris: Plon.
Boyd, L. H., Jr., and G. Iverson (1979) *Contextual Analysis: Concepts and Statistical Techniques.* Belmont, CA: Wadsworth.
Butler, D. and D. Stokes (1969) "The influence of a local political environment," pp. 144-150 in D. Butler and D. Stokes (eds.) *Political Change in Britain.* New York: St. Martin's Press.

Coleman, J. S. (1964) *Introduction to Mathematical Sociology.* New York: Free Press.

Converse, P. E. (1962) "Information flow and the stability of partisan attitudes." *Public Opinion Quarterly* 26: 578-599.

Cox, K. R. (1969) "The voting decision in a spatial context," in C. Board, R. J. Charley, and P. Haggett (eds.) *Progress in Geography: International Reviews of Current Research* (Vol. 1). London: Edward Arnold.

——— (1974) "The spatial structuring of information flow and partisan attitudes," in M. Dogan and S. Rokkan (eds.) *Social Ecology.* Cambridge, MA: MIT Press. (Originally published in 1969.)

Davis, J. A. (1966) "The campus as a frog pond: an application of the theory of relative deprivation to career decisions of college men." *American Journal of Sociology* 72: 17-31.

Durkheim, E. (1951) *Suicide* (J. A. Spaulding and G. Simpson, trans.). New York: Free Press. (Originally published in 1897.)

Erbring, L. and A. A. Young (1979) "Individuals and social structure: contextual effects as endogenous feedback." *Sociological Methods and Research* 7: 396-430.

Eulau, H. and J. W. Siegel (1980) "A post-facto experiment in contextual analysis: of day- and night-dwellers." *Experimental Study of Politics* 7: 1-26.

Finifter, A. W. (1974) "The friendship group as a protective environment for political deviants." *American Political Science Review* 68: 607-625.

Green, B.S.R. (1971) "Social area analysis and structural effects." *Sociology* 1: 1-19.

Hauser, R. M. (1970a) "Context and consex: a cautionary tale." *American Journal of Sociology* 75: 645-664.

——— (1970b) "Commentary and debate: Hauser replies." *American Journal of Sociology* 76: 517-520.

Homans, G. C. (1961) *Social Behavior: Its Elementary Forms.* New York: Harcourt Brace Jovanovich.

Isambert, F. A. (1960) "Enterrements civils et classes sociales." *Revue Française de Sociologie* 1: 298-313.

Kadushin, C. (1979) "Frontiers of research in network theory and method." Prepared for delivery at the AAAS Meetings, Houston, Texas, January 5. (Center for Social Research, CUNY Graduate Center, New York.)

Laming, D. (1973) *Mathematical Psychology.* London: Academic Press.

McClosky, H. and H. E. Dahlgren (1959) "Primary group influence on party loyalty." *American Political Science Review* 53: 757-776.

McPhee, W. N. (1963) "Note on a campaign simulator," in W. N. McPhee (ed.) *Formal Theories of Mass Behavior.* London: Macmillan.

——— and J. Ferguson (1962) "Political immunization," in W. N. McPhee and W. A. Glaser (eds.) *Public Opinion and Congressional Elections.* New York: Macmillan.

McPhee, W. N. and R. B. Smith (1962) "A model for analyzing Voting Systems," in W. N. McPhee and W. A. Glaser (eds.) *Public Opinion and Congressional Elections.* New York: Macmillan.

McPhee, W. N., with R. B. Smith, and J. Ferguson (1963) "A theory of informal social influence," in W. N. McPhee (ed.) *Formal Theories of Mass Behavior.* London: Macmillan.

Menzel, H. and E. Katz (1955-1956) "Social relations and innovation in the medical profession: the epidemiology of a new drug." *Public Opinion Quarterly* 19: 337-352.

Merelman, R. M. (1968) "Intimate environments and political behavior." *Midwest Journal of Political Science* 22: 382-400.

Miller, W. E. (1956) "One-party politics and the voter." *American Political Science Review* 50: 707-725.

Miller, W. L. (1978) "Social class and party choice in England: a new analysis." *British Journal of Political Science* 8: 257-284.

Orbell, J. M. (1970) "An information-flow theory of community influence." *Journal of Politics* 32: 322-338.

Przeworski, A. (1974) "Contextual models of political behavior." *Political Methodology* 1: 27-61.

Putnam, R. D. (1966) "Political attitudes and the local community." *American Political Science Review* 60: 640-654.

Segal, D. R. and M. W. Meyer (1974) "The social context of political partisanship," in M. Dogan and S. Rokkan (eds.) *Social Ecology*. Cambridge, MA: MIT Press. (Originally published in 1969.)

——— and S. H. Wildstrom (1970) "Community effects on political attitudes: partisanship and efficacy." *Sociological Quarterly* 11: 67-86.

Sprague, J. (1981) "A measurement improvement experiment using contextual information from census data." Prepared for delivery at the annual meeting of the Midwest Political Science Association, Cincinnati, April 15-18. (Political Science Paper 68, Washington University, St. Louis.)

——— and L. P. Westefield (1979a) "Campaign and context interaction." Prepared for delivery at the annual meeting of the Midwest Political Science Association, Chicago. (Political Science Paper 32, Washington University, St. Louis.)

——— (1979b) "An interpretive reconstruction of some aggregate models of contextual effects." Prepared for delivery at the annual meeting of the Southern Political Science Association, Gatlinburg, Tennessee. (Political Science Paper 41, Washington University, St. Louis.)

Tingsten, H. (1937) *Political Behavior: Studies in Election Statistics*. London: P. S. King. (Authorized facsimile of the original book by University Microfilms, Ann Arbor, Michigan.)

Valen, H. and D. Katz (1964) "Political change and stability in the Stavanger area," in Henry Valen and Daniel Katz (eds.) *Political Parties in Norway*. London: Tavistock.

5

Methodology Versus Ideology

The "Economic" Approach Revisited

BRIAN BARRY

The genesis of this chapter is best described in the following way. A long time ago (it now seems) I wrote a book entitled *Economists, Sociologists, and Democracy* (1970) in which I contrasted two distinctive methods of analyzing democratic institutions. One, which I dubbed the "economic," corresponded roughly to what may be called the "rational-choice" approach. The other, which I labeled (with, perhaps, less justification) the "sociological," was constituted by the then-regnant approach of structural-functionalism, as exemplified especially in the works of Talcott Parsons and his followers.

The substance of the book consisted of detailed critical discussions of characteristic products of these two schools. This discussion was, however, sandwiched between two more general chapters. In the introductory chapter I drew attention to the contrasting ideological origins of the two approaches, the economic approach coming out of an individualist, rationalist, utilitarian outlook, and the sociological approach tracing its origins to the European reaction against just those tendencies.

In the conclusion I asked whether, in the light of the preceding discussion, one had to conclude that the ideological tendencies were inseparable from the two approaches or whether they could be detached from them. I argued that they could and should be emancipated from their ideological origins.

Some months after accepting the invitation to give a lecture at Indiana University on a methodological topic, I began to wonder what problem I should address. It occurred to me that it might be interesting, after a decade or so, to reopen the question of the relation between methodology and ideology. In that period we have seen many attacks from different angles on the idea of ideological neutrality—not merely in the social sciences but also in the citadels of positivism, the physical and biological sciences. We have also had another ten years of experience with the actual practice of the economic approach. The sociological approach has melted away (who now reads Parsons?), but the rise to a greater prominence of the economic approach makes it even more important to ask whether or not it can, in principle, be an ideologically neutral instrument of social research.

The answer that I shall offer is a cautious yes. I think that there is nothing in the root assumptions of the economic approach that forces it toward predetermined conclusions about politics and society. At the same time, I must concede that as practiced it has generally lent support to certain crassly individualistic liberal political beliefs that are endemic in American culture. The fit is so comfortable that one is naturally driven to ask oneself if the popularity of the economic approach in the United States derives precisely from this conformity with fundamental beliefs rather than from its intrinsic merits as an explanatory system. I strongly suspect this is so. To square that with the answer given earlier, I suggest that it is not the basic ideas of methodological individualism that are ideologically loaded, but the specific interpretations of them that are followed in most of the work within the tradition of rational-choice theorizing.

I shall try to establish this for the case of analyses of the workings of representative government, and in particular, the "political business cycle" literature. Before doing that, I shall say something about methodological individualism as a general thesis in the philosophy of the social sciences. There are, in fact, rather compelling reasons for thinking that adequate explanations of social phenomena must operate by showing how these phenomena arise out of the interactions of the consequences of decisions made by individual actors.

THE ADVANTAGE OF ECONOMICS

Let us begin by asking why economics is a more highly developed social science than any other. My answer is that economics takes for itself an easier set of problems than the other social sciences, one that lends itself more easily to formalization and to the development of a deductive system.

The sense of "easiness" relevant here is illustrated by a story I recall reading (though I forget where) about a world-famous theoretical physicist taking up the study of economics and pronouncing after a few weeks that it was "too difficult." The difficulty of economics, for someone like that, does not of course lie in its theoretical structure but in the extraordinary complexity of the phenomena in relation to the comparative simplicity of the theory. To the highly trained mind of a physicist, the project of economics must have appeared akin to laying out the gardens of Versailles in the middle of a tropical rain forest.

As economics is to physics, so is the rest of social science to economics. In the obvious way in which economics is "easier" than physics—roughly speaking, that it is not so easy to prove that somebody does not know what he is talking about—the rest of social science is even easier. And, conversely, in the deeper and more interesting sense in which economics is more difficult than physics, the rest of social science is more difficult still: the phenomena more varied and mixed up together, lending themselves less well to treatment within a unified and tractable theory.

In accounting for the relative sophistication of economics by adducing the more amenable subject matter, I am, of course, taking a position that is open to challenge. An alternative

explanation that I have observed to find favor among economists is that economists are brighter than other social scientists.
The fact is not one that I would wish to dispute. What I dispute
is its relevance. It is quite true that economics has in its history
attracted a handful of powerful analytical minds of the general
type of the best physical scientists (though not probably of
quite the same caliber) and that no other social science can say
the same. But the point is that people with this kind of capacity
for abstract thought would have been wasted in any other social
science because there is simply not the same scope for building
grand theoretical structures that actually illuminate reality. Certain kinds of intellect, in other words, are attracted to economics because it lends itself to their talents; it is not that
economics is the way it is because people with those talents
happened to go into it, and that, if the same people had
happened to go into sociology or political science, those disciplines would now be as sophisticated as economics.

I cannot undertake to consider all the alternative reasons that
might be offered for the relative success of economics in coming
up with a deductive system that seems to connect in some way
with reality. I shall simply present the explanation that seems
plausible to me. It happens to have been given first by John
Stuart Mill in Book VI, Chapter IX, Section 3 of the *Logic*
(1961), but I do not wish to claim that it should be believed
simply because of that. I do think, however, that Mill's ideas on
the methodology of the social sciences are worth resuscitating,
not out of a spirit of deference to authority but on their own
merits. At times Mill sounds rather quaint, as in the seriousness
with which he takes people like Comte and Buckle. But there is
a lot of good sense in Book VI of the *Logic* all the same.

It may appear odd that I should talk about resuscitating Mill,
for two reasons. First, there is the general revival of interest in
him, evidenced by the (almost absurdly comprehensive) edition
of his collected writings, which is now almost completed, and
the large number of books and articles that have been devoted
to him in the past decade. The other, more particular, reason is
that "everybody knows" that Mill recommended the famous

methods of agreement and difference as the basic tools for investigation in the social sciences.

Informal and unsystematic opinion polling among social scientists whom I know has suggested that, among those who claim to know anything on the matter, Mill is thought to have endorsed the methods of agreement and difference. (The other two analyzed in the same context—concomitant variations and the method of residues—seem to have dropped out of the general consciousness, but they might be said to presuppose the first two.) We can also find Mill invoked in print as the patron saint of the comparative method in the social sciences. An illustrious recent example is Theda Skocpol's *States and Social Revolutions*, where we read that the "logic [of comparative historical analysis] was explicitly laid out by John Stuart Mill in his *A System of Logic*" (1979: 36). The reference here is not to Book VI but to Book III, Chapter VIII (n. 91, p. 302), where Mill introduces the methods of agreement, difference, concomitant variation, and residues in the context of the physical sciences. Skocpol then goes on to outline the methods of agreement and difference and relate them to her own work (1979: 36-37). An eminent political scientists, Harry Eckstein, has even gone as far as to say, in a methodological chapter on "Case Study and Theory in Political Science," in the *Handbook of Political Science*, that "the disanalogies between experiments in physics and comparative studies in politics are so great as to make one wonder how the comparative observation of unmanipulated cases could ever have come to be regarded as any sort of equivalent of experimental method in the physical sciences" (1975: 117). And he says that one of "the main reasons . . . by my reading [is] the influence of J. S. Mill's *Logic*" (1975: 117).

Eckstein may be correct in attributing to the influence of Mill's *Logic* the belief among social scientists that comparison is an adequate alternative to controlled experimentation. But if so, a cruel irony is at work here. Mill's chapter (Book VI, Chapter VII) "Of the Chemical, or Experimental, Method in the Social Science" is entirely devoted to arguing the contrary: that, precisely for the kinds of reasons set out by Eckstein in his article, the comparison of naturally occurring changes or differences is almost entirely lacking in the kind of probative value given by experimentation in the physical sciences. In other words, this is one of those cases in which what "everybody knows" is the flat opposite of the truth. If this chapter succeeds in doing nothing else, I hope that it will at least dispel the myth that John Stuart Mill recommended the methods of agreement and difference for use by social scientists.

Mill's reasons for rejecting the use of inductive methods in social science were set out most succinctly in his general discussion of these methods in Book III of the *Logic*. The key is what he calls "plurality of causes," the impossibility of separating out single cause-effect relations by observation. In "The Phenomena of Politics and History," Mill (1961: 298) says,

> Plurality of Causes exists in almost boundless excess, and effects are, for the most part, inextricably interwoven with one another. To add to the embarrassment, most of the inquiries in political science relate to the production of effects of a most comprehensive description, such as the public wealth, public security, public morality, and the like: results liable to be affected directly or indirectly either in *plus* or in *minus* by nearly every fact which exists, or even which occurs in human society. . . . Nothing can be more ludicrous than the sort of parodies on experimental reasoning which one is accustomed to meet with, not in popular discussion only, but in grave treatises, when the affairs of nations are the theme. "How," it is asked, "can an institution be bad, when the country has prospered under it?" "How can such or such causes have contributed to the prosperity of one country, when another has prospered without them?" Whoever makes use of an argument of this kind, not intending to deceive, should be sent back to learn the elements of some one of the more easy physical sciences. Such reasoners ignore the fact of Plurality of Causes in the very case which affords the most signal example of it.

It may be said, of course, that the kind of casual empiricism criticized by Mill here is a far cry from the elaborate and sophisticated comparative efforts of, for example, Barrington Moore, Jr., Stein Rokkan, Charles Tilly, Arend Lijphart, Juan

Linz, or Theda Skocpol. And I would certainly not want to deny the value of such work. Nevertheless, Mill's basic methodological point is still valid: Society-level generalizations always have far fewer cases to deal with than the number of plausibly relevant differences between those cases. Events like the occurrence of revolutions, the breakdown of democratic regimes, or the creation of consociational democracies are rather infrequent. It seems almost inconceivable that (even if they are really sufficiently homogeneous sets of outcomes to be worth trying to explain) it will be possible to come up with a really compelling set of necessary and sufficient conditions. It will always be possible for someone to suggest alternatives that are compatible with the evidence, and the evidence will never be sufficient to settle the issue. This is not, to repeat, any reason for denigrating such macrosocial studies, but it does provide a strong incentive for the search for an alternative way of going at things. Let us, then, follow Mill along the next steps in his own argument.

Our text here is Book VI of the *Logic,* which is devoted to the social sciences, or perhaps behavioral sciences since psychology is included. (Mill's term is "moral sciences.") The inductive methods (agreement and difference, and so on) are rejected in Chapter VII. Chapter VIII is also negative in its effect. Mill here proceeds to the demolition of another false method, which he calls the "Geometrical, or Abstract Method." This is associated with his father's *Essay on Government* and similar efforts in deductive political analysis. I shall return to this discussion below, since it has a considerable bearing on my own theme, which is precisely the limitations of deductive political analysis. For now, however, let us press on to Chapter IX, where we finally get the right answer, which is "the Physical, or Concrete Deductive Method."

There is no need to delve too far into the details of Mill's conception of this method. It is similar to the familiar hypothetico-deductive method as we have received it in a more elaborate form from Hempel, Nagel, Popper, Braithwaite, and other logical positivists or fellow travelers of the logical positivists in this century. The basic idea (and I am, of course, putting this crudely) is that we construct theories, deduce from them concrete implications, and test these implications against reality. In the light of the outcome, we regard the theories as supported or disconfirmed. In the latter case, we seek to modify the theories.

Mill, however, presents a different angle from the orthodox Hempelian or Popperian approach that I have just outlined. Whereas the Hempel/Popper school has no theory about where hypotheses come from (something they regard as a question for the psychology rather than the logic of scientific discovery), Mill suggests that the materials for deduction are to be drawn from the study of simple cases, by a process of induction. The deductive stage then consists of combining laws drawn from simple cases so as to apply them to complex ones. The stage of verification consists of seeing how well the results of the deduction compare with the actual phenomenon. It probably helps to understand what Mill has in mind here, to recognize that his paradigm is Newton's explanation of the elliptical orbits characterizing planetary motion by deducing them from the law of gravity, which had been established on the basis of simple terrestrial experiments.

This was, of course, the archetype of successful scientific explanation for people in the eighteenth and nineteenth centuries. One might say that Mill appears to have tailored the whole category to fit this one case. Certainly, Mill's other examples are less spectacular and at times seem rather forced. But the underlying idea seems quite sound. Insofar as he departs from the Hempelian formula, that is to his credit.

A well-known difficulty with the Hempelian "covering-law" theory of scientific explanation is that it calls any generalization that covers the case in hand an explanation, even if only by saying, "This kind of thing always happens." But the production of a generalization of this kind is not what we normally have in mind when we call for an explanation of a phenomenon in terms of something "more basic." We want an explanation in terms of "deeper" causes—mechanisms, structures, what you will.

Thus, saying that the function of hemoglobin is to distribute oxygen around the body is saying nothing except that this is what it does, plus the suggestion that it is beneficial to the human body for it to happen. That this kind of statement can be fitted into the framework of a Hempelian covering-law explanation simply illustrates what is wrong with the covering-law conception. In contrast, Perutz's work on the structure of hemoglobin (see Judson, 1979) genuinely explained the operation of the hemoglobin molecule by showing how, by changing from one shape to another, it is able to pick up and offload oxygen atoms. (It is, incidentally, a perfect illustration of cultural lag that the heyday of functionalist social science, which drew its paradigm from a teleological rather than a mechanical model of biological explanation, coincided with the rise of molecular biology in the 1950s and 1960s.)

All this, however, is a mere skirmish. The important question for our present purpose is what implications the method has for the study of society. In spite of the fact that only the last of the six books of the *Logic* addresses itself to the "moral sciences," this was the important question for Mill too; indeed, he took up the project of writing the book out of a concern about the reactionary implications of Whewell's work on scientific method. According to Mill, then, the only general laws available are what he sometimes calls "laws of human nature" and at other times refers to as "psychological and ethological laws." (Psychology is "the science of the elementary laws of mind"; ethology, "the ulterior science which determines the kind of character produced in conformity to those general laws, by any set of circumstances, physical and moral" [1961: 567].) Putting these "laws" to work on social phenomena, we may be able to establish "tendencies":

> We may be able to conclude, from the laws of human nature applied to the circumstances of a given state of society, that a particular cause will operate in a certain manner unless counteracted; but, we can never be assured to what extent or amount it will so operate, or affirm with certainty that it will not be counteracted; because we can seldom know, even approximately, all the agencies which may

co-exist with it, and still less calculate the collective result of so
many combined elements [1961: 585].

Even then

It would, however, be an error to suppose that, even with respect to
tendencies, we could arrive in this manner at any great number of
propositions which will be true in all societies without exception
[1961: 586].

Hence,

The deductive science of society will not lay down a theorem,
asserting in an universal manner the effect of any cause; but will
rather teach us how to frame the proper theorem for the circumstances of any given case. It will not give the laws of society in
general, but the means of determining the phenomena of any given
society from the particular elements or data of that society [1961:
586].

We may, indeed, as Mill suggests in the following chapter (X,
"Of the Inverse Deductive, or Historical Method"), be able to
establish empirical trends, but we cannot use them with any
confidence as a basis for prediction unless we have reason to
expect the underlying conditions to remain unaltered.

The big question raised by all this, obviously, is whether
social phenomena lend themselves to the creation of widely
applicable deductive systems or whether each historical
sequence has to be explained by appealing to some unique
concatenation of circumstances, such that the move away from
these to the outcome can (with any luck) be brought under
some set of individual-level regularities. The latter possibility
leaves a very limited role for the social sciences. Yet, if it is all
that is available, it would be absurd to reject it in the pursuit of
something more ambitious but actually useless. An example
would be the case put forward by Donald Moon, in his chapter
in this book. Why did the Swedish Social Democrats alone
employ demand-management policies in the 1930s? Because
their leaders had become persuaded that these policies had a

chance of working and nothing else had. The kind of psychological generalizations needed to fill out this explanation are, it is
plain, pretty banal. So it is easy to see why the explanation was
criticized, as Moon reports, on the ground that it was "not
theoretical." But it may be the explanation for all that.

Under what conditions can more complex deductive structures be raised without completely losing contact with the
actual phenomena to be explained? Here, again, I find Mill's
ideas in Chapter IX of the *Logic* helpful, though incomplete.
According to Mill, the precondition is that the "immediately
determining causes" of a set of phenomena should be simple
and stable. Thus, economics can "reason from [the] one law of
human nature" that "a greater gain is preferred to a smaller"
(1961: 587). Even then, however, Mill (1961: 593) says—and
this seems correct—that it will be possible only to deduce from
theory the general direction of the effect of some policy (such
as an import tariff), and there will still be room for disagreement about the net effect of policies with different tendencies.

Politics stands in the most extreme contrast with economics,
in Mill's view. The reason that there can be no deductive science
of politics on the same lines as economics is that "the qualities
of the particular people and of the particular age" are "mixed
up at every step" with the institutions ("forms of government"
and the like; *Logic,* 1961: 591). The institutions affect the
characters of the people and the characters of the people affect
the working of the institutions. The kind of simplification
achieved in economics by positing a simple universal motivation—the desire for material gain—is not therefore open to the
political scientist.

In this context, it is useful to go back to Mill's objections to
politics as an example of deduction from a simple set of causes
in his discussion of the so-called geometrical method. This is, in
effect, the physical method misapplied to cases where the
phenomena are in fact too complex to be sensibly explained in
such simple terms. Mill's primary reference here is to his father's
Essay on Government and the increasingly acrimonious and
tedious discussion that followed it between Macaulay and various philosophical radicals.[1] The conclusion, stated in the *Logic*

and repeated in the *Autobiography,* was that the *Essay on Government* should have been put forward as a polemic in favor of extending the suffrage, and not as a firm deduction from universally valid principles. For example, James Mill's axiom that governors will always seek their own interest is simply not something that is true in all times and places. Its degree of approximation to the truth varies from time to time and place to place, and we can, in principle, hope to say something about the determinants. The general conclusion that Mill draws from his criticism of the geometrical method runs as follows:

> It is unphilosophical to construct a science out of a few of the agencies by which the phenomena are determined, and leave the rest to the routine of practice or the sagacity of conjecture. We either ought not to pretend to scientific forms, or we ought to study all the determining agencies equally, and endeavour, so far as it can be done, to include all of them within the pale of science; else we shall infallibly bestow a disproportionate attention upon those which our theory takes into account, while we misestimate the rest, and probably underrate their importance [1961: 583].

Thus, Mill's claim about the special features of economics, with which I said I concurred with some qualifications, is that economics is the study of an aspect of social life in which one can get further than elsewhere by assuming a handful of simple motivations. These include that people prefer to pay less rather than more for the same commodity, to be paid more rather than less for the same job, to get more interest rather than less on their savings if the security is equal, and so on. The point is, as Mill correctly says, that if we content ourselves with assertions about tendencies rather than precise predictions, we may be able to do quite well using only these banal generalizations about human behavior. For example (to take a contemporary illustration), we can anticipate that there will be a withdrawal of deposits from savings and loan associations if money market funds pay higher interest, even though we cannot say with any confidence how fast the rate of withdrawal will be or how far the rundown will eventually be.

NONECONOMIC APPLICATIONS

The question then naturally arises at this point: Are there other aspects of social life that lend themselves to a similar kind of abstract treatment? Here my qualification comes into play, since I think that there are. The way to proceed seems to be to work out, as Mill suggested, theories that can be seen to be true when appropriately simple conditions are satisfied, and then extend them in a somewhat ad hoc way to more complex, real-life cases. Good examples of this can be found, I suggest, in the analysis of problems of collective action. The basic theorem of the theory of collective action is, I take it, pretty familiar. The standard modern reference is Mancur Olson's *The Logic of Collective Action* (1965), but the idea itself was familiar, for example, to Hobbes and Rousseau.[2] The basic notion is that situations can exist such that if each person pursues his or her individual interest, the outcome is one that all the participants like less than an attainable alternative if they had all done something different. The typical example is the nonprovision of a public good in the absence of "selective incentives" (Olson's term).

Let me illustrate the way in which this simple idea has been fruitfully taken up in a couple of recent books. The first example is Samuel Popkin's *The Rational Peasant* (1979). Popkin makes use of the theory, as put forward by Olson, in an exotic setting: Vietnamese peasant society. Looking at his subject from an Olsonian perspective, he sees peasants as beset on all sides by problems of organizing collective action that would be mutually beneficial if everyone played his or her part, in a context where formal sanctions are unreliable. Some inefficient arrangements are, he suggests, tolerated just because the more efficient alternatives would require unattainable feats of collective action. Thus, plots are not consolidated because the only way for individual peasants to avoid the threat of being wiped out by highly localized bad conditions would be for the village to set up some sort of insurance scheme, and this requires too much trust. Similarly, collective granaries are not introduced because nobody is trusted to run them. And mutual aid groups (for planting and harvesting, for example) have to be kept small to avoid "free riders." Other features of peasant societies can be explained by presenting them as ingenious ways of circumventing problems of collective action. Thus, if each person is made responsible for a specific task failure to perform which will destroy the whole enterprise, each has an interest in doing his or her bit, provided that the value to each individual of the collective benefit outweighs his or her own cost of contribution.

Popkin (1979: 254) also observes that people may contribute to a public good (a revolution, for example) because they believe in it and want to take part on a basis of "ethics, altruism, or conscience," even if the Olsonian calculus would favor passivity. He speculates that in such cases what is most important in encouraging participation is the expectation that the movement will be effective, and suggests that anything that demonstrates the steadfastness and incorruptibility of the leaders will tend to raise the confidence of potential followers.

Popkin's achievement is this: He insists on taking the provision of collective goods as problematic and refuses the easy and invalid move of assuming that some piece of collective action is explained simply by pointing out that it is mutually beneficial to the parties for it to occur rather than not occur. By worrying about the way in which public goods get provided, Popkin is led to frame good questions. He is led to look at hitherto unexamined phenomena by being sensitized by the theory of collective action to anticipate their existence.

This second example is Russell Hardin's *Collective Action* (1982). This is, among other things, a superb exposition of the basic problem of collective action as posed by Olson and synthesis of subsequent theoretical work. For our present purpose, however, the aspect that I want to concentrate on is Hardin's work in refining the basic Olson theory. That theory predicts that public television will never have subscribers, unless some immensely wealthy person regards it as worth his while personally to underwrite its costs in his area, and it similarly predicts that the only people to join the Sierra

Club will be those attracted by its "selective benefits," such as trips. Yet, both of these predictions manifestly fail to fit the facts. Why? Among other possibilities, he canvasses a revised motivational assumption. Olson had taken as his assumption that people will consult only their own costs and benefits in deciding whether or not to contribute to the provision of a public good. But suppose people are willing to contribute their "fair share" so long as (enough) others do so too. How could such a norm come about, and how could it be sustained? In the last half of this book, Hardin tries to give answers. He thus introduces a more complex theoretical apparatus to show how, in favorable circumstances, it may be possible to solve a collective-action problem without the kinds of "selective incentives" invoked by Olson.

These examples seem to me to illustrate the development of a research program within the general spirit of Mill's concrete deductive method. We have a rather simple theory, based on a deduction from premises that specify particular relations and motivations. We then move from that in two directions: First, as with Popkin, we look for phenomena embedded in highly complex total situations that the simple theory helps explain. Second, as with Hardin, we take relatively simple counter-examples, and we try to extend the original theory so as to account for them.

Notice, incidentally, I am not suggesting that the theory could be made to explain all social phenomena by a further series of extensions. It remains a theory about problems of collective action. Not all phenomena in the world exhibit (still less consist wholly in) problems of collective action.

These seem to me to represent first-rate examples of successful social science. The collective-action framework is, in the Lakatosian terms borrowed by Donald Moon, a progressive research program. What about the charge that the tradition of methodological individualism is inherently biased politically? We need to make clear what the charge is before we can assess its force. This issue is not a simple left/right one. We have only to consider that the roll call of anti-individualists would include de Maistre and Durkheim—a Catholic reactionary and a staunch supporter of the Third Republic—to see that this would be too crude. Rather, the suggestion is, I think, that the approach of methodological individualism encourages a vision of human beings as isolated creatures capable of being moved only by appeals to their self-interest, which is somehow extrasocially defined.

The charge can, I believe, be rebutted. As a general approach, methodological individualism insists only that there must *be* adequate individual motivations to sustain whatever pattern of social cooperation is postulated. It does not have any built-in assumptions about the range of possible motivations or their inherent fixity. It is, surely, a tautology that any social arrangement must somehow generate the motives in people to play the parts ascribed to them. If such a tautology brings up short certain kinds of utopian engineers of communal living, all that shows is that not everybody thinks clearly. But since the failure to consider individual motivation means that one is building on sand, it is hard to see why any reasonable person should object to the reminder that any polity, association, or organization must find a way of providing people with reasons for doing what they have to do.

Having said that, however, I must at once concede that in practice there is a tendency to specify the motivational assumptions in a way that is loaded. This is illustrated in the present instance by the original statement of the collective-action problem as put forward by Olson, where a rather simple-minded assumption of universal self-interest was made. But, as we have seen in the brief discussions of the later work of Popkin and Hardin, this assumption can fruitfully be relaxed. We are still left with the core insight that there are usually inadequate *self-interested* reasons for contributing to a collective good derived from the difference one's contribution will make, without thereby having to suppose that the only alternative is some other way of tapping self-interest.

The conclusion is, then, that there is nothing wrong with the methodology *in general terms.* The general idea of putting together processes that can be observed to occur in simplified

instances to explain real-world events is fine. The trouble lies in
the choice of premises and the exclusion of extraneous factors,
even if these are in reality important. If, in Michael Oakeshott's
terms, an ideology is an "abridgement of a tradition," then we
can say that these oversimplified models may function as
ideologies in a somewhat analogous sense.

AN IDEOLOGICAL APPLICATION

I shall conclude this chapter by presenting an example of the
way in which, it seems to me, the basic ideas of methodological
individualism have been employed for ideological purposes,
namely the models of a politico-economic electoral cycle that
have been produced in the last decade or so. Theories of the
interaction between a competitive electoral system and a
market economy have been developed by a number of economists, using the standard kind of modeling techniques used in
economics.[3] These theories are designed to explain the existence of a "political business cycle" a cyclical pattern of inflation and recession timed so that the optimal mix coincides with
election times—or to explain why the process of electoral competition operates in a perverse way to generate a greater amount
of inflation than voters want.

Economists who venture into the formal analysis of politics
tend to share similar assumptions about the motivations and
capacities of political actors. Politicians are assumed to be
conscienceless seekers of power, those in office being prepared
to inflict any amount of damage on their countries in order to
increase, however fractionally, their share of the vote. At the
same time, they are assumed (at any rate, for the purpose of
model-building) to be consummately skillful at manipulating
the levers of economic policy in pursuit of the end of reelection. Voters, by contrast, are assumed to have barely any
cognitive or ratiocinative capacities at all. They are barely even
able to remember the economic record of the current government when election time comes round. Moreover, they have
absolutely no ability to anticipate the future (or if they do,

then somehow this anticipation does not affect their actions). These zombies react (within the limits set by their defective memories) to past experience of inflation and unemployment rates with approval or disapproval, and also perhaps to the direction in which those rates are changing, but they do not attempt to make any estimates of their future course and respond to them.

If these are the premises, it is hardly surprising if the conclusion turns out to be that democracy is a flawed form of government. What could anyone expect from a system characterized by a group of rogues competing for the favor of a large collection of dupes? No wonder economists from the South Side of Chicago find Santiago more congenial than Washington as a place in which to give advice to policymakers!

Contrary to Milton Friedman's notorious "methodology of positive economics," no deductive system can be better than its premises. Yet, this methodology seems to infect even those who would repudiate Friedman's economics. Characteristically, the premises are baldly stated in the politico-economic models developed by economists, and little discussion of the plausibility is offered.[4] It is also noticeable that only anecdotal evidence at best is normally adduced in support of the conclusions. All the effort is lavished on working out the model. This emphasis on technical virtuosity at the expense of the realism of the premises or the accuracy of the predictions is, it would appear, deeply embedded in the reward structure of the economics profession.

Without going deeply into the matter here, let me suggest that these assumptions do not appear to approximate the truth for any democratic country. Studies of national-level politicians in democratic countries tend to suggest that they are motivated either by policy concerns or service of a personal kind to their constituents (see Putnam, 1973). If you like, you can say that these are "satisfactions of office," but the point to bear in mind is that the satisfaction is derived not merely from holding office, but from doing something with it that is thought to be worthwhile. Moreover, although those in government of course wish to be reelected, other things being equal, political leaders are often highly motivated by the thought of their reputations in history, and may well be unwilling to pay a price of ignominy for doing something with predictably bad consequences in order to secure some short-run electoral gain. Even Nixon, by his subsequent attempts to justify himself, illustrates the importance of reputation to politicians.

Voting studies suggest that voters are not the Skinnerian pigeons of the usual economist's model. They try to decide which candidates would do better on the issues that they care most about and tend to vote according to the answers they come up with.[5] They also try to form estimates of the competence of alternative candidates, which is something that takes us way beyond the picture of voters merely responding to the "goodness or badness of the times" by voting for the ins or the outs.[6] If voters nevertheless sometimes find it hard to make a clear judgment about the policy differences between candidates, this need not reflect their stupidity but rather the reluctance of politicians to go beyond generalities and say what they would do when faced with a hard choice. When the politicians differentiate themselves clearly on an issue, the evidence suggests that voters are usually aware of it (see Page, 1978).

As far as the shortness of memory is concerned, there is indeed no lack of evidence that voters give more weight to the more recent performance of the economy, but if we start from the presumption that they are trying to use the information they have in order to decide whether or not to entrust the government with another term in office, that does not seem an unreasonable thing to do. After all, for the first year in office, or even the second, a government can blame troubles on its predecessors with some legitimacy. The longer it has been in office, the better the case for using the current state of the economy as a basis for judging its priorities and capabilities. Where responsibility can be fixed clearly, voters apparently have long enough memories: President Ford's pardon of Nixon came right down at the beginning of his term of office, for example. Those who disapproved of it seem to have had no difficulty in holding Ford responsible and remembering it at election time. The more pessimistic analyses of democratic political economy imply that a government might find it advantageous to stage a massive deflation in its first two years if it could get the unemployment rate down again and combine it with a lower rate of inflation by election day. But I think this illustrates the disadvantage of thinking in terms of an electorate with a memory that decays at a rapid rate. That kind of gratuitous deflation would, I predict, be remembered because it would be important information about the way the government worked. The Republicans, to give the most obvious example, were distrusted by many people for a whole generation because of what 1929-1932 was taken to have told their complacency in the face of mass unemployment.

What is perhaps equally remarkable is the spottiness of the evidence in favor of the existence of a "political business cycle." One might say that it has something of the status of a myth—something that *must* be the case, whatever the evidence says, so that supporting cases are seized on and disconfirming ones finagled away.[7]

Another commonly held article of faith is that there is "too much" inflation in democratic countries. This belief has no necessary connection with that in the "political business cycle," though it is often held concurrently with it. The thesis was even put forward by some economists in the 1970s that democratic governments will *never* act so as to bring down the rate of inflation—a thesis that has clearly been disproved. Governments, in fact, seem to act against inflation when it gets unpopular enough, which is presumably what one would predict on the basis of the standard rationale of representative government. Given the great economic and social costs of combatting inflation by the orthodox techniques usually favored by these same economists, it is hard to see why reluctance to use them should be regarded as a sign of the failure of governments to act in accordance with the preferences of their electorates. One might suggest that governments in a number of countries (including the United States, Britain, Switzerland, and West Germany) have recently sacrificed far too much in terms of unemployed people and resources in quest of a reduced inflation rate.

The reason for treating these analyses by economists as ideological is simply that they are in fact for the most part politically motivated. The use of tendentious assumptions about the workings of democratic regimes is designed to lay the groundwork for schemes of all kinds to hobble the elected governments and take central economic decision-making functions out of their hands.

We would be totally naive to ignore the wider political context of proposals to require balanced budgets, to fix the money supply automatically according to some formula, to go back to the gold standard, to make central banks more autonomous, and so on. The economists who make such proposals are, for the most part, economic liberals in the nineteenth-century sense. That is to say, they believe that collective action carried out through the state should be kept to a minimum and that the market should determine what gets produced and who receives what income. There is, as both defenders and critics of the market have been forced to recognize over the last hundred years or so, a built-in tension between liberalism (in the nineteenth-century sense) and democracy. Almost a century ago, Sir Henry Maine (1886) made the point in *Popular Government,* a work whose continued relevance is vouched for by the recent decision of the Liberty Press to reprint it. W.E.H. Lecky (1896) carried the argument further and injected a greater note of stridency in *Democracy and Liberty* (also recently reprinted by the Liberty Press). The same ideas inform the view of their descendants, the so-called Mont Pelerin group, including such figures as von Mises, Hayek, and de Jouvenal.

Monetarism, and, more generally, market liberalism, are inevitably going to be betrayed by democratic governments sooner or later. For the workings of the market are not, in fact, conducive to the well-being of the majority of the population. Any government concerned with reelection finds itself intervening, whatever its official doctrine, to cushion people from the effects of unconstrained market forces. The demand-management, guidelines, statutory controls over wages and prices, and other devices that governments use in order to try to moderate inflation are simply an aspect of this general phenomenon.

Anyone whose primary commitment is to the market must, therefore, look upon the democratic state, with its inevitable tendency to regulate, make collective provision, and redistribute, with antipathy. The political problem facing such a person is, of course, how, in a democratic state, to get democratic approval for tying the hands of elected governments in perpetuity. These problems do not, of course, arise in nondemocratic regimes, and it is not therefore surprising that it is territories with authoritarian regimes, such as Hong Kong, Taiwan, and South Korea, that are the apple of the market economist's eye.

The beauty of inflation is that it can be used as a rallying cry to sweep up people who might otherwise be chary of plans to cripple the ability of governments to make economic policy. A perfect example is provided by James Buchanan, a leading proponent on the balanced-budget constitutional amendment. For a decade before he attached his wagon to the inflationary star with *Democracy in Deficit* (Buchanan and Wagner, 1977), he was calling for a "constitutional counterrevolution" to undo the work of the New Deal and the Warren Court.[8] Anti-inflationary hysteria is an opportunity to mobilize behind proposals that would, in calmer times, be widely recognized as reactionary twaddle. *That* is, in the end, the most important reason for worrying about inflation.

CONCLUSION

I do not wish to oversell the significance of methodological discussions of the kind I have been engaged in here. What mainly determines the fate of a method is its success or failure in generating good work. The decline of structural functionalism and systems theory occurred not only because of the logical potshots that I and others took at them, but also because they did not seem to give a handle on interesting problems. If they had, the logical weaknesses would no doubt have been patched up over time. By the same token, methodological individualism may be logically impeccable, but it will be adopted as an approach only if it is seen to deliver.

In this chapter, I have been concerned primarily with clearing away misconceptions that may otherwise prejudice the case for methodological individualism. I have in particular suggested that the ideological slant so often found in "rational-actor" models is not inherent in the method itself but arises from the specification of the motives and the capabilities of the actors that are incorporated into the model. With a richer specification we can reasonably expect more plausible and less ideologically loaded results. But there is no way of saying in advance how wide a range the method will encompass. That depends partly on the nature of things and partly on the degree of ingenuity and persistence shown by the users.

NOTES

1. Reprinted in Lively and Rees (1978).

2. Rousseau's grasp of the essential points is brought out well by Oakerson (1980).

3. See Nordhaus (1975), MacRae (1977), Wagner (1977), Lindbeck (1966), Parkin (1975), Sjaastad (1976), Buchanan and Wagner (1977), and Brittan (1975, 1977a, 1977b).

4. Some economists are so infatuated by their premises that they apparently come to regard them as self-evident. Thus, the coauthor of *Democracy in Deficit*, Richard E. Wagner, wrote in a paper on "Economic Manipulation for Political Profit" (1977: 396-397): "Once it is recognized that macroeconomic policy is made by self-interest, not disinterested or other-interested politicians, a new perspective on macroeconomic policy appears, particularly if politicians believe that economic conditions can affect their survival prospects." That politicians are self-interested (read: concerned only to stay in office) is not something to be "recognized"; it needs to be argued for and is, I am suggesting, quite implausible.

5. For a relatively early study, see Key (1966), and for recent analysis of the 1972 election in these terms, see Popkin et al. (1976).

6. Popkin et al. (1976) show convincingly how much McGovern was hurt by perceptions of lack of competence following the Eagleton affair.

7. An extensive analysis would be out of place here. In Barry, forthcoming, I show the weakness of the evidence put forward by Nordhaus (1975) and Tufte (1978).

8. See Buchanan (1975, 1977) and my review article on these two books (1980). (1980).

REFERENCES

Barry, B. (1970) *Economists, Sociologists, and Democracy* London: Collier-Macmillan. (Reprinted in 1978 by the University of Chicago Press as a Phoenix edition, with a new introduction and an updated bibliography.)
——— (1980) Review of *The Limits of Liberty: Between Anarchy and Leviathan* and *Freedom in Constitutional Contract: Perspectives of a Political Economist. Theory and Decision* 12: 95-106.
——— (forthcoming) "Does democracy cause inflation?" in L. Lindberg and C. Meier (eds.) *The Politics and Sociology of Global Inflation.* Washington, DC: Brookings.
Brittan, S. (1975) "The economic contradictions of democracy." *British Journal of Political Science* 5: 129-159.
——— (1977a) "Can democracy manage an economy?" in R. Skidelsky (ed.) *The End of the Keynesian Era.* New York: Holmes & Meier.
——— (1977b) *The Economic Consequences of Democracy.* Part IV: Economics and Democracy. London: Temple Smith.
Buchanan, J. M. (1975) *The Limits of Liberty: Between Anarchy and Leviathan.* Chicago: University of Chicago Press.
——— (1977) *Freedom in Constitutional Contract: Perspectives of a Political Economist.* College Station: Texas A&M Press.
——— and R. E. Wagner (1977) *Democracy in Deficit: The Political Legacy of Lord Keynes.* New York: Academic Press.
Eckstein, H. (1975) "Case study and theory in political science," pp. 79-137 in F. I. Greenstein and N. W. Polsby (eds.) *Handbook of Political Science* (Vol. 7). Reading, MA: Addison-Wesley.
Hardin, R. (1982) *Collective Action.* Baltimore: Johns Hopkins University Press for Resources for the Future.
Judson, H. F. (1979) *The Eighth Day of Creation.* New York: Simon & Schuster.
Key, V. O. (1966) *The Responsible Electorate.* Cambridge, MA: Harvard University Press.
Lecky, W.E.H. (1896) *Democracy and Liberty.* London: Longman.
Lindbeck, A. (1966) "Stabilization policy in open economies with endogenous politicians." *American Economic Review* 66, 2: 1-19.
MacRae, D. (1977) "A political model of the business cycle." *Journal of Political Economy* 85: 239-263.
Maine, H. S. (1886) *Popular Government.* New York: H. Holt. (Reprinted by Liberty Press/Liberty Classics, 1977.)
Mill, J. S. (1961) *A System of Logic, Ratiocinative and Deductive.* London: Longman.
Nordhaus, W. D. (1975) "The political business cycle." *Review of Economic Studies* 42: 167-190.

Oakerson, R. J. (1980) "The unity of the represented: Rousseau's contribution to the theory of constitutional choice." Working Paper W80-1, Workshop in Political Theory and Policy Analysis, Indiana University, Bloomington.

Olson, M. (1965) *The Logic of Collective Action.* Cambridge, MA: Harvard University Press.

Page, B. I. (1978) *Choices and Echoes in Presidential Elections.* Chicago: University of Chicago Press.

Parkin, M. (1975) "The politics of inflation." *Government and Opposition* 10: 189-202.

Popkin, S. L. (1979) *The Rational Peasant: The Political Economy of Rural Society in Vietnam.* Berkeley: University of California Press.

——— et al. (1976) "What have you done for me lately?" *American Political Science Review* 70: 779-805.

Putnam, R. (1973) *Beliefs of Politicians: Ideology, Conflict, and Democracy in Britain and Italy.* New Haven, CT: Yale University Press.

Sjaastad, L. A. (1976) "Why stable inflations fail: an essay in the political economy," pp. 73-86 in M. Parkin and G. Zis (eds.) *Inflation in the World Economy.* Manchester: Manchester University Press.

Skocpol, T. (1979) *States and Social Revolutions.* Cambridge: Cambridge University Press.

Tufte, E. (1978) *Political Control of the Economy.* Princeton, NJ: Princeton University Press.

Wagner, R. E. (1977) "Economic manipulation for political profit." *Kyklos* 30: 395-410.

6

Interpretation, Theory, and Human Emancipation

J. DONALD MOON

It is commonly believed that a scientific discipline must have a widely shared set of standards that it uses to evaluate research. Without such standards, there would be no way of making rational judgments about the value of scientific work, nor would practitioners be able to choose and organize their own projects in a rational way. From this perspective, one of the major shortcomings or problems of political science is the apparent confusion and diversity of standards in our field. I say "apparent confusion" because I have not done the systematic research that would be needed to demonstrate this claim. But there is no lack of impressionistic evidence that supports it.

The diversity of schools and "approaches" and their frequent debates over the correct method to study politics are powerful indications of a lack of consensus on such standards. This dissensus shows itself in such mundane matters as the reviewing process that professional journals use to select articles for publication. It is not uncommon for one to submit a manuscript to a journal, only to receive one very critical set of comments and one that is full of praise. The frequency of such occurrences is

149

evidence of a lack of agreement on standards of good scientific work.

I might also mention the study of Richardson and Somit (1980) that reviewed the work of the dissertation awards committees of the American Political Science Association. These committees are supposed to select the best dissertation in a particular field for a given year. Richardson and Somit discovered that few of the awards these committees made went to individuals who subsequently established an impressive record of published research. This finding does not demonstrate that the awards committees made poor judgments, but it shows that we have at least not rewarded people who would pursue successful programs of research.

One of the reasons we experience a confusion of standards in our discipline is that political scientists employ at least two different forms or models of explanation, which give rise to two different sets of criteria or standards of evaluation. One model is essentially theoretical, explaining political phenomena in terms of general laws and theories. The other model, which I will call the "intentionalist" or "interpretative" model, explains political phenomena in terms of factors specific to the case at hand. Because research based on the intentionalist model does not invoke general laws or theories, it is not viewed as adequate by adherents of the theoretical model. Intentionalists, on the other hand, are experts at demonstrating the failure of theoretical explanations to account for the "facts" of particular cases.

In the face of such disagreement, what strategies are open to us? One possibility is to reconstruct the intentionlist model in such a way as to show that it is, in actuality, a special case of the theoretical model. It has often been claimed that interpretative explanations, while not *appearing* to rely upon general laws and theories, must implicitly make use of them if they are to be cogent. While this is a popular position, I will argue that it is inadequate. The attempt to reconstruct intentionalist explanations as theoretical accounts ends up by trivializing the theoretical model itself, and it does so because of properties inherent in our conceptualization of human action. This argument is a focus of the next two sections of this chapter.

A second strategy, one associated with a number of philosophers of social science (see Louch, 1969; Winch, 1958), is to abandon the theoretical pretensions of political science altogether. This is a position that has had very little, if any, appeal to practicing political scientists, and for good reason: The interpretative model is by itself an inadequate basis of political inquiry. Important types of political phenomena can be explained only by going beyond the confines of the intentionalist model and constructing explanations that are essentially theoretical in form, as I will show below.

If political science is necessarily theoretical, might we then dispense with the intentionalist model altogether? For if it cannot be reconstructed to accord with the theoretical model, and if the theoretical model is essential to certain types of political inquiry, could we not extend it to cover all aspects of political inquiry, and thereby have one model of explanation, and only one set of standards governing political research? In the last section of the chapter, I argue against this proposal—not on the grounds that it is impossible, but on the grounds that it does not accord with what I take to be an important reason for undertaking political research in the first place. Ultimately, retaining both the intentionalist and the theoretical models is justified by a commitment to human freedom, and to a conception of politics as at least potentially a sphere of collective self-determination.

THE INTENTIONALIST MODEL OF EXPLANATION

An Example

I would like to present the intentionalist model by means of a particular example. At the 1980 meeting of the American Political Science Association, an exchange occurred at a panel over how to explain the policy responses of different governments to the Great Depression.[1] In particular, some governments adopted a policy of demand stimulation. Others followed more restrictive policies, attempting to balance their national budgets and maintain the value of their currencies. No obvious relationship exists between regime type and policy choice; Germany and Sweden both pursued demand-stimulation policies, while Britain did not. Moreover, the British Labour party did not support such policies, while the Swedish Social Democrats did. Now how is this to be explained? In particular, focusing on the last example of Swedish Social Democrats and British Labourites, we see that both operated in a democratic political system, both were parties of the left with close trade union ties, and both represented constituencies that were deeply hurt by the depression. How do we explain the differences in their responses?

One of the participants presented an explanation that was quite similar to the account offered by Hugh Heclo in his study of *Modern Social Politics in Britain and Sweden* (1974). In outlining this position, I will follow Heclo's argument. Heclo's book won the Woodrow Wilson Award in 1975, and in commending the book, Samuel Huntington wrote that it "represents a major contribution to the discipline on not one but several fronts and stands as a model of how political scientists can tease out of history answers to the question: why?"[2] One of the things that is notable about Heclo's explanation is its lack of systematic theory, which is evident in his account of the differences between the reaction of the Labour party and the Swedish Social Democrats to the Great Depression. Indeed, Heclo's principal explanation for the policy differences between these groups is that the Swedes, unlike their British counterparts, came to adopt a different account of the operation of a capitalist economy from that of classical economics. According to the classical doctrine, secular unemployment was impossible in a market economy because disequilibrium in the labor market would lead to declining levels of wages, and so to employers hiring more workers. This should continue to the point where all workers who are willing to work at the prevailing wage were employed. Government policies, such as support for the unemployed, would generally tend to interfere with this mechanism by, for example, keeping wage rates artificially high, and so would exacerbate the very problems they were meant to relieve.

Throughout the 1920s, according to Heclo, virtually all political actors accepted the classical account of a market economy, and the prescription of a balanced government budget that it entailed. Thus, all found their freedom of action to be extremely narrow in dealing with social problems such as unemployment, poverty, old age, and illness. Programs to relieve these problems were drastically limited by available government revenues, and by the fear that the programs would end up making the problems worse by exacerbating unemployment. While Labour and Social Democratic parties would press for some liberalization of existing programs, they could scarcely make or advocate significant changes so long as they accepted the parameters of economic debate given by the classical theory. When in power, left-wing governments regularly failed to deliver even on their liberalization policies, because they had to bow to supposed "economic realities."

But in the early 1930s the Swedish Social Democrats broke out of the straight-jacket of classical economic doctrine and accepted a kind of Keynesian account of economic stability. Ironically, the Social Democratic leader Wigforss and his colleagues were helped to an alternative view of the economy by their study of the policies and arguments presented by the British Liberal Party in 1928. The adoption of the Keynesian doctrine freed government policy from the constraints of a balanced budget and so widened the range within which government policy could be formulated. Rather than being helpless in the face of widespread unemployment, the government could henceforth pursue an active policy of demand management to create full employment. The government was also freed from the budget constraints that prevented its adopting policies to secure other social goals such as old-age pensions and protection against illness. Because the Social Democrats, like their British counterparts in the Labour Party, were committed to these goals, the period following their adoption of a new set of beliefs about the economy was characterized by extensive policy innovation in these fields. But because the leadership of the British Labour Party at the time did not accept the new theories, their policies were stuck in the same rut that had characterized all of the parties during the 1920s.

The Practical Syllogism

Now this account, I think, captures the essence of Heclo's argument. His analysis, of course, is more complex and detailed; in particular, he describes the actual processes through which the new policy goals came to be adopted through the formation of coalitions with different political groups in Sweden, and he analyzes the dissenting viewpoints within the various political parties involved. But the key argument he makes is that the change in economic doctrine was decisive and explains the differences between the British and Swedish cases at this time.

The logical structure underlying this explanation is that of the practical syllogism, or practical inference. That is, we explain the actions in question by laying out the reasoning process that led to them. This requires that we specify the goal or purpose the actors wished to achieve, in this case economic stability with full employment, and their beliefs about what is required to achieve this purpose. From these premises we infer that the actor does, or sets out to do, the required action. The general form of the practical syllogism is something like the following:

- A wishes to bring about Y.
- A believes that to bring about Y he or she must do X.
- A does (or sets out to do) X.

This explanation scheme is incomplete in a number of ways, and it must be qualified by specifying the actor's other purposes and the consequences of doing X for these purposes. Obviously, A will only do X if A believes that the value of achieving Y outweighs the other purpose A must give up or postpone in order to do X. But even if we add these qualifications, this explanation scheme does not directly invoke general laws, or lawlike statements of any kind.

This was immediately evident at the panel meeting to which I referred above. As soon as the explanation was presented, a member of the audience got up to criticize it on the grounds that it was not theoretical. Rather than depending for its explanatory force on general laws, its explanatory force comes from the way in which it arranges the particulars of the case. What is important in this account is what Wigforss and his associates thought, how they balanced such purposes as ameliorating the conditions of the working class in capitalist society versus bringing about a socialist revolution, the kinds of arguments that led them to reject the classical model of multimarket equilibrium, and the information they had about the effects of different kinds of policies. Such explanations gain in verisimilitude not by invoking general theories about policymakers' responses to economic dislocation, but by showing how further particulars of the case, and especially particulars regarding the goals and beliefs of the actors, fit into an account of their behavior that enables us to see the point of what they did, that enables us to make sense of their actions.

CRITICISMS OF THE INTENTIONALIST MODEL

Are Intentionalist Explanations Really Nomological?

Now, in response to the charge that intentional explanations are not theoretical, we could do several things. One appealing tack is to argue that these explanations are not complete as they stand, and that they must be supplemented by a general law linking a person's holding certain goals and beliefs with that person's subsequent action. After all, it might be argued, this way of explaining a person's actions in terms of his or her reasons implies that these reasons were the cause of the person's actions, that it was because he or she had just those reasons for acting that he or she acted in the manner indicated. But according to a common view of "causation," to say that some event X is the cause of some event Y is to say that events of type X are constantly conjoined with events of type Y. Thus, a causal account necessarily presupposes a generalization linking the cause and the effect.

The argument over reasons and causes is one of the most sharply debated issues—I would say nonissues—in the philosophy of social science recently. So in order to avoid the thicket, let us grant that an agent's having certain reason are the causes of his or her acting in a certain way, and let us also grant that causal explanations rest upon general, lawlike statements. Does this cause us to revise anything I have just said about intentional explanations? Especially, does this challenge my point that intentional explanations do not invoke general laws, and that their explanatory power rests upon the way in which they arrange the particular facts of a specific case? I will argue briefly that these points remain valid in spite of our granting that reasons may be the causes of actions. To see this I would like to consider one attempt to supplement the account of the practical inference I gave with a generalization, which would make it conform to the covering-law model.

In an excellent study of the theory of action, Alvin Goldman (1970: 73) offers the following statement as an example of the sort of generalization linking reasons and actions:

If any agent S wants to do A' (at t) more than any other act, and if S believes that basic act A_1 is more likely to generate A' than any other (incompatible) basic act, and if S is in standard conditions with respect to A_1 (at t), then S does A_1 (at t).

This "generalization" is refined in his discussion, but the refinements do not really affect my argument. Therefore I will concentrate on this simple example. It seems to me that Goldman's putative generalization points to a crucial feature of intentional explanations. They presuppose what we might call a principle of rationality. We can explain what an agent does in terms of one's reasons only if we think that the agent is rational, that there is a close relationship between what a person does and the person's reasons for doing it. Indeed, that is implicit in the concept of having a "reason" for action in the first place! If, to mention the extreme case, the person's movement were due to a physiological reflex, there would be no question of explaining the action in terms of "reasons" at all.

When I say a "principle of rationality," I do not mean that all intentional explanation is a form of the rational-choice model, as it is known in political science, or any other specific conception of rational behavior. The standards we use in assessing an action as "rational," as appropriate to the actor's situation and purposes, are themselves variable and may be culturally and institutionally specific. But even if the standards we use are themselves subject to interpretation, and even if they vary from place to place and time to time, we must be able to use them to see the point of an action, to see it as coherent with an agent's purposes, beliefs, and principles, if we are to understand it at all as a piece of intentional behavior.

It is because intentional explanation presupposes some principle of rationality that generalizations such as Goldman's appear to be trivial and redundant. Even if it is not, strictly speaking, a tautology, it simply specifies the assumption of rationality that is presupposed by intentional explanation in the first place. Adding it to the practical syllogism does not make any significant difference to this pattern of explanation. In particular, it does not serve to make accounts such as Heclo's any more theoretical. Thus, it does not help to still the objection that was made to it at the APSA panel.

Even if we make the most generous assumption and agree that Goldman's "generalization" is a scientific law, it has the peculiar property that it explains *all* intentional actions. Like some modern garments, it can be advertised with the slogan, "One size fits all," as it stretches to cover the facts of any particular case. But this just means that the real explanatory work must be done by the particulars in each situation. Political science, at least as it concerns explaining intentional action, along with all of the other social sciences, becomes nomologically complete. All that is left to us is to reconstruct the reasoning processes of actors in each particular situation, add Goldman's Law, and we have another triumph of the covering-law model. But we have no theory—this law stands alone—and no theoretical progress.

Intentionalist Explanations and the Hermeneutic Circle

Even if my argument that Goldman's Law will not get us anywhere is accepted, it might be argued that we should nonetheless persevere in the attempt to reconstruct intentional explanations as nomological explanations. But I would like to suggest that this very enterprise is not apt to succeed. That is because of the way in which we use the idea of rationality in understanding human actions. A moment ago I suggested that Goldman's Law might be construed as a tautology. Strictly speaking, it is not a tautology, for someone could in some sense "want" to bring about Y more than anything else, could in some sense "believe" that the most likely or even the only way of doing so would be to do X, and yet still not do X. But how would we respond to this description of a person's behavior? At the very least we would want to know more about the situation. Perhaps the object the person wants is forbidden by a moral or religious injunction, and the person forswears it, even though wanting it very badly. In this case, we recognize that the meaning of "want" must be clarified. If we understand "want" in its most general sense to include a person's sense of duty, then we could say that the person does not actually want Y more than anything else, but rather wants to observe this moral imperative more than he or she wants Y.

In a second case we might find that the person believes that doing X would also produce Z, which the person highly disvalues. Revising our description of the situation, we once again find the behavior to make sense. Finally, we might consider a third possibility. It turns out that the person is deeply depressed, and sits about listlessly, unable to act at all, even to achieve the things he or she most "wants" when doing so is within the person's capabilities. Hearing this, we are apt to conclude that the person's not doing X was not an intentional action (or, rather, forbearance). In this case, we would deny the applicability of the scheme of intentional explanation to the behavior in question, and conclude that a different pattern of explanation would be required to deal with a person suffering from this condition.

This discussion is necessarily highly schematic, but I think it is sufficient to bring out an important feature of this mode of explanation: that our interpretation of a person's beliefs, wants, and actions are interdependent in the sense that we attribute a particular belief or want or action to a person only in relationship to the person's other beliefs, wants, or actions, in such a way as to bring about a maximal degree of coherence among them. This, of course, is an instance of the famous interpretative or hermeneutic circle: The meaning of a part can only be understood by placing it within the context of the whole, and the whole can only be interpreted in terms of the meanings of the parts. In the case of human actions, beliefs, and purposes, we attempt to make sense out of someone's actions by interpreting each aspect in the light of the others, and thus stand prepared to revise our judgments of any specific aspect when we find it does not cohere with others. Thus, in viewing ostensibly puzzling behavior, we might revise our understanding of what a person wants, or the person's beliefs, or even our judgment that a person's actions were intentional, as we did in the cases I presented a moment ago.

Because of this feature of action explanations, they only come to have verisimilitude when they bring together a significant number of facts about an actor's situation, beliefs, attitudes, and other actions—that is, by the way in which they arrange the particulars of the case. Because there are so many degrees of freedom, so to speak, this kind of account is plausible only when the case is presented with great richness of detail. It is by weaving together this richness of detail in a coherent story that the interpretations will be cogent. But this makes it unlikely that we will be able to formulate nontrivial generalizations linking beliefs, values, and actions. Because the significance of any particular belief, value or action depends upon the role it occupies in relationship to the actor's other ideas and actions, statements relating ideas and actions come to be so detailed that they end up applying only to a particular case, and so lose their standing as generalizations. On the other hand, if the dangers of overparticularization are avoided, one usually finds the opposite error. Ideas and actions are characterized in such general terms that statements linking them become vacuous. This dilemma is well known to political scientists. So much of the empirical work we do is of the case-study variety. In comparative politics the tradition of area studies is still strong. It is a common frustration with case studies of, say, administrative decision-making, or rural development in Gambia, that they leave us drowned in details, or benumbed by sterile generalizations, or often both at once. This is true even though such studies generally involve explaining political and social phenomena that are not intentional actions, and which lend themselves much more to theoretical treatment.

Intentionalist Explanations
and Causality

I have conceded that explanations of actions in terms of the agent's reasons for action are a species of causal explanations, but I have been arguing that intentional explanations are not nomological, in the sense that they do not make use of general laws. This is not an inconsistent position. As Donald Davidson (1970) has argued, to say that a person's having certain reasons caused the person to act in a certain way requires that there be a general law linking those two events. But the law need not link those events under the description of these events as reasons and actions. For example, my wanting and believing that getting Y requires that I do X may be an instance of a particular neurophysiological state whose general designation is NS. My doing X may, in this case, involve my arm's rising through the contraction of certain muscles, which, let us say, is identical to neurophysiological state NSB. Thus, if there is a general law, "Under certain conditions, if NS, then NSB," the intentional explanation of my action in terms of my reasons will be backed up by a causal law linking these two events—but under quite different descriptions. Instead of generalizing about reasons and actions, the law would generalize about neural states and muscle movements. But because in this particular case my having certain reasons is also describable as my being in a particular neural state, and my performing a certain action is also describable as the motion of certain muscles and nerves, the intentional explanation of my action is also a causal explanation.

If this is so, it might be argued that we should just dispense with intentional explanations altogether, and develop accounts utilizing the descriptive language that is suitable for the development of such causal laws. Indeed, it might be thought that this argument opens the way to a reductionist approach that might put us out of business! But both these points are mistaken. Any possible "reductionism" would not be straightforward because the two descriptive vocabularies may divide the world in radically dissimilar ways. If what I said above about intentional descriptions is correct, they almost surely will. In the example I have been using, suppose that y is having my candidate elected, and x is voting for my candidate, and that one votes by raising one's arm at a particular point. Now if the election procedure were changed, so that instead of raising one's arm, one dropped a marble into a box, then we would presumably require a different causal law linking my purposes and beliefs, on the one hand, and my action, on the other, because my voting for my candidate is no longer an instance of neurophysiological state NSB. In other words, the same reasons and the same actions may be linked by any number of different causal laws on different occasions, and the different reasons and different actions may be linked by the same causal laws! Even if we knew the microprocesses and relations that determine behavior, so that knowing a person's brain state we could predict the person's muscle movements perfectly, we may be unable to say what the person is thinking, nor what action will be performed. I should add that my argument does not show that there is no one-to-one relationship between types of neurophysiological states and types of mental states, but only that the possibility of the kind of causal explanation I have been discussing does not require such a relationship. If what I said above about the contextual nature of our ascriptions of ideas and actions is correct, it would seem that any such relationship between brain states, or muscle movements and actions, would be most improbable.

EXPLAINING SOCIAL INTERACTION

So far I have been arguing that intentionalist explanations do not make use of general laws, and so are not theoretical, at least not in ways involving general laws.[3] The significance of this argument might be doubted, however, on the grounds that such explanations do not figure prominently in political science. While we do occasionally focus on the actions of a particular individual, we generally are interested in political phenomena that involve interactions among different people and therefore cannot be viewed as an intentional performance of any one person. But in many cases such phenomena can, as it were, be decomposed into a specific sequence of actions, each of which changes the situation faced by other actors, given their own particular values and purposes. Their actions in response to this changed situation can then be explained, and the way in which their responses change the situation of the first actor can be seen. This type of account, which von Wright (1971: 135ff.) calls "quasi-causal" explanations, can be used to explain fairly complex kinds of social interactions by tracing out singular causal relationships that hold in a particular context, and enabling us to see how actions can come to have unintended effects without moving outside of the intentionalist paradigm. It is a kind of causal analysis, because it shows how one event brings about or leads to another; but we can call it only quasi-causal because the links in the chain are made up of intentional actions and the effects of these actions on the situation faced by other actors. In general, we have no idea of what laws, if any, underlie these particular relationships. In any event, we provide such explanations without offering any such laws. If the argument I presented above is at all plausible, it is quite possible that our having full knowledge of the microlaws and processes governing human behavior would be of no help in making these explanations.

Practical Inferences and
Causal Relationships

One of the reasons one might think that intentional explanations are necessarily of very limited scope arises from the structure of such explanations themselves. In this scheme, an action is explained as following from an individual's desire to achieve a certain end, together with his or her belief that performing the action in question is the best way to do so. This belief, it might be thought, must be a belief about what causal relations actually hold in the world: the belief, "if I do x, then y will occur," could only be true if actions of type x cause events or situations of type y to occur. Thus, intentionalist explanations of social behavior implicitly refer to causal relations that hold among social and political phenomena, and thus our attention could be better spent discovering and analyzing these relationships, which would lead us in the direction of developing general theories.

It is natural for us to draw such an inference, and while this argument makes an important point, it is seriously overstated. Somewhere Wittgenstein once said that problems in philosophy arise from a diet of one-sided examples, and that is what has happened here. Many social and political actions are not purposive in the sense that this argument requires, and some actions that are purposive rely not so much upon causal regularities to achieve their effects, but upon institutional rules. Many of the things that we do are not purposive in that the effect we intend to achieve in the performance of the action is achieved simply in the performance of the action itself. Expressive or symbolic behavior is an obvious case in point. When I raise the flag outside my house on the Fourth of July, I intend to express my patriotism, and I achieve that effect in raising the flag. Expressing patriotism is not an effect of raising the flag as, for example, an explosion is an effect of igniting gunpowder that has been compressed into a container. Rather, expressing patriotism is the meaning or part of the meaning of the action itself.

In the case of actions that are purposive in the sense that their purpose lies outside this action itself, I may not rely upon causal regularities to achieve the effects I desire so much as relying upon institutional rules. When I say to you, "Please pass the salt," I intend to get you to pass me the salt. But I do not expect to achieve that result because I believe that there is a causal connection between uttering these sounds and receiving salt, but because I rely upon your understanding the meaning of my utterance and your responding to it in accordance with a social convention that you accept. Similarly, when I vote for candidate A with the intention of affecting the outcome of the election in A's favor, I am relying upon the conventions or rules of the institution of elections in our society to achieve this result. When candidate A is elected because he or she received a majority of the votes, it is not because "receiving a majority of the votes" and "being elected" are causally connected, but because "receiving a majority of the votes" *constitutes* "being elected" or means "being elected" under the conventions of our electoral institutions.

Let me hasten to add that in this analysis I am not arguing that these events are exempt from the realm of causality, that my receiving the salt or my candidate's assuming office are, somehow, uncaused events. The occurrence of these events depends upon certain actors performing certain actions or forbearances—my dinner partner's passing the salt, the generals not calling out the troops—and these actions or forbearances, being events in the world, no doubt are causally explicable under certain descriptions. All I am saying is that in performing

these actions I am, as it were, invoking conventions that norma-
tively require certain responses on the part of others. When my
action fails to achieve its intended effect, it does not mean that
my beliefs about causal relationships are in any way wrong; it
may simply mean that the actors in question have violated these
rules. If I am relying upon any generalization or regularity, it
may be something to the effect that the people currently
subject to the rules or conventions in question generally conform to them. Such a generalization is hardly explanatory; at
best, it might provide grounds for forecasting or expecting the
behavior in question, but certainly not for explaining it, in the
way that the theoretical model explains phenomena.

Sometimes one might engage in purposive behavior intending
to bring about a certain effect not by means of an institutional
rule or practice (though such rules may be involved), but by
directly affecting the choices available to a particular individual,
or by communicating information to the person which affects
the person's beliefs or values in a determinate way. In this kind
of situation I may be relying upon general causal regularities
governing human behavior, but I may also be relying upon my
knowledge of the particular persons involved and other particulars of the situation.

In a recent study reevaluating the presidency of Eisenhower, Fred Greenstein provides a number of political examples
in discussing what he calls Eisenhower's "hidden hand leadership" (1979-1980: 584-586). For example, when Eisenhower
persuaded congressional leaders to hold hearings on Senator
Joseph McCarthy's "conduct in a fashion that would vitiate
McCarthy's usual means of defending himself against counter-
attack," or when he arranged to have one of his own spokesmen
respond to an attack on the Republican party for its
"McCarthyism," he was engaged in a systematic campaign "to
end McCarthy's political effectiveness." But in deciding on what
would be effective in weakening McCarthy, Eisenhower did not
appear to invoke generalizations about political influence and
its determinants so much as to rely upon knowledge of
McCarthy's particular purposes and techniques. It was because

of the use that McCarthy made of the media, for example, that it was important to prevent his gaining access to it as much as possible. And he was prevented access by deliberately forbearing actions that would have led to McCarthy's having an occasion to make statements that the media would have carried as news, and by persuading the networks to give access to others in preference to McCarthy.

It is in situations such as these that quasi-causal analysis is most at home. That is because the pattern of social interaction they involve can be grasped without moving outside the intentionalist paradigm. But social action can be purposive in a third way, in that instead of relying upon singular causal relations to bring about the desired effect, an actor may rely upon generalized causal relations. This, of course, is the type of action I discussed at the beginning of this chapter, for party leaders during the 1930s in Britain and Sweden explicitly held general theories of the economy that, as we have seen, accounted in part for their policy decisions. While an intentionalist perspective may be capable of explaining the actions people take because they accept certain theories, it is incapable of comprehending such theories themselves, in the sense that one could not develop, test, or assess such theories within the context of the intentionalist research program. This is because such generalized theories do not explain social phenomena as the outcome of action and reaction sequences of specific individuals, as is the case with quasi-causal relationships. Although it may be obvious that all social phenomena are ultimately constituted by the actions of individual men and women, the patterns that characterize complex structures of human interaction cannot, as a practical matter, always be discerned by tracing the effects of one person's actions upon another's situation, the second person's response to this changed situation, the effects this response has on yet a third person, and so on. A case in point might be the multiplier effect of a change in government expenditures, where the impact of each successive round of additional spending quickly becomes swamped by the other factors operative in the economic system. As long as one is confined to the study of identifiable individuals and the model of singular, quasi-causal relations, one might never even develop a conception of the "multiplier effect" that one might then try to demonstrate empirically. Thus, when it comes to explaining what might be called "systemic events," the intentionalist model is no longer adequate.

EXPLAINING SYSTEMIC EVENTS: THE STRUCTURE OF POLITICAL THEORIES

An important part of the work of political science and the other social sciences is to discover the causal regularities that characterize such systems of interaction. These regularities may be explained by positing "typical" individuals and their relationships, as opposed to particular identifiable persons. While this abstraction from the concrete individual puts us outside of the interpretative framework, it does so in a way that does not negate it, because our posited "typical" individuals are still intentional agents, who are assumed to act on the basis of their beliefs and objectives, and their behavior must been seen to be "rational" at least in a broad sense. But for the purposes of theory construction, we abstract from the particular context of their beliefs and objectives, and set out to explain the patterns that characterize social interaction in terms of general assumptions about (1) the kinds of beliefs, values, and capacities individuals have, and (2) the typical relationships they have with each other. That is, we construct models of social and political structure that we people with individuals to whom we have imputed certain kinds of beliefs, values, and capacities. We can then use these models to analyze the impact that particular actions or events will have on the pattern of interactions, and to discover the causal regularities that determine these outcomes.

In speaking of "typical" individuals and their relationships, I should guard against a misunderstanding. I am not suggesting that social theorists are free to fabricate whatever assumptions they want to make about human beings, nor that these assumptions are exempt from empirical testing and checking. Enough has been said about the inadequacies of the approach to theory construction, represented best perhaps by Milton Friedman's "methodology of positive economics," that holds that the truth of one's basic assumptions is not important to the truth of one's theories, and I shall not repeat these arguments here. It is only when actual individuals hold the types of beliefs and values and have the kinds of capacities we impute to them that our theories are genuinely explanatory. While we are free to abstract from the specific content of their beliefs or situations, this is only because the particular content is not necessary in order to explain the systemic events and regularities in question.

I would like to stress that these two components of a social or political theory are equally crucial. The set of assumptions constituting our typical individual we may call a "model of man," or a "conception of human behavior," and the set of assumptions we make about their relationships we might call a "model of social structure" or, to use Norbert Elias's (1978) suggestive term, a "figuration." Neglecting either of these components leads to a serious misunderstanding of the nature of social theory, the way in which social theory is explanatory, and in particular the nature of social laws. Elias (1978: Ch. 3), for example, stresses the autonomy of social science and its nonreducibility to psychology. He argues that the charac- teristics of the social system are the essential determinants of social phenomena, and that it is easier to explain individual behavior in terms of the characteristics of the system than to explain the characteristics of a social system in terms of the behavior of individuals. He presents a series of models designed to show that the distribution of power within a social system depends critically upon the number of actors and their figura- tion, rather than upon the psychological characteristics of the actors. But in order to reach this result he must tacitly make certain assumptions about human behavior—for example, that individuals who possess things needed by others will attempt to use their possession to control the behavior of others. To spell out this assumption and provide some grounds to it would pretty quickly require one to make a number of claims about human beliefs, objectives, and capacities.

If structuralists are guilty of suppressing their own assumptions about human behavior, individualists often neglect the critical role of structural assumptions in their theories, and so misunderstand the nature of the laws their theories support. This is particularly true of adherents to the rational-choice paradigm, who see the assumption of rationality as crucial and tend to ignore the figurative assumptions involved. In his foreword to Downs's *Economic Theory of Democracy*, for example, Stanley Kelley writes, "Downs assumes that political parties and voters act rationally in the pursuit of certain clearly specified goals—it is this assumption, in fact, that gives his theory its explanatory power" (Downs, 1957: x). But this very statement makes reference to the figurational assumptions of Downs's theory; the assumptions about political structure implicit in the use of terms like "voters" and "political parties" are as important and as essential to the theory's explanatory power as is the assumption of rationality. Similarly, in his excellent study of microeconomics, Alexander Rosenberg (1976) focuses on putative laws governing the behavior of individual economic agents and, not surprisingly, sees the postulate of rationality to be central to (though not exhaustive of) microeconomic theory. But even such ostensibly individualist claims as the statement that two commodities are substitutes for a particular consumer involve essential reference to structural factors in the use of concepts such as "commodites," "income," and even "consumer." The standard statement of the substitution effect in economic analysis presupposes the existence of an advanced money economy, if not a full-blown market in consumer goods.

Because social theories of this sort rest upon these two sets of assumptions, a model of behavior and a model of social structure or figuration, the causal regularities these theories support may not have all the characteristics of scientific laws. In particular, it may be impossible to formulate the behavioral or the figurational assumptions in such a way as to yield causal regularities that can be expressed as unrestricted universals. This would occur, for example, if these assumptions made essential reference to practices or concepts that were embedded in an essential way in a particular culture or form of life. In that case, the generalizations the theory supported would apply only to particular periods in time. Despite appearances, they would not be unrestricted universals.

This, I take it, is one of the central criticisms that Marx (1844: 120) directed at the political economy of his day.

> Political economy begins with the fact of private property; it does not explain it. It conceives the material process of private property, as this occurs in reality, in general and abstract formulas which then serve it as laws. It does not comprehend these laws; that is, it does not show how they arise out of the nature of private property.

Because economists begin with the assumption of private property, which they tacitly assume to be an unalterable feature of human condition, they erroneously believe that the laws their theory supports must govern all possible societies: Being general laws, they must specify "boundary conditions" to which all social life must conform. But, Marx argues, private property is historical—it is a characteristic of a particular form of society, so the laws of political economy are not universal in scope. Moreover, because private property is historical, because it develops at a particular point in time, the task of an adequate social theory is to explain how it comes into existence and the conditions under which it might be transcended. That, of course, was to be Marx's own project.

WHY KEEP THE INTENTIONALIST MODEL?

I have been arguing that the intentionalist model of explanation is not, by itself, a sufficient basis for political inquiry. Much of what political scientists study cannot be explained using the interpretative framework, and we must therefore employ the model of theoretical explanation. Moreover, I have contended that the intentional model cannot be reduced to the theoretical model, and that having two models of political explanation is one reason we have conflicting standards for evaluating political research. The obvious question these conclusions lead to is, Why not abandon the intentionalist model altogether?

I would like to begin to answer this question by considering one justification for retaining the intentionalist perspective that I believe to be wrong. This justification might be called the ontological position, because it holds that the intentionalist perspective is required by the nature of political and social phenomena. These phenomena are, the argument goes, constituted by the intentional performances of human beings, and have the character and identity they have because of the ideas and self-understandings of these people. You cannot, for example, recognize something as an "election" or an act of "voting," except in terms of the ideas and self-understandings of the actors involved. A given set of performances is an election only if this accords with the meaning it has for the participants. This argument is by now familiar to all of us, and I do not mean to say that it is entirely mistaken. What it does is to bring out a feature of the *language* we use to individuate political phenomena, to recognize political actions and events as of a certain type. As students of politics we invariably, without exception, adopt a language for describing and identifying our material that commits us to the intentionalist perspective because it is, in the first instance, the language of the social and political actors we are studying.

It is from this fact that the peculiar hermeneutic problems of the human sciences arise, the necessity to grasp the meanings of ideas, actions, symbols, and cultural artifacts in terms of the self-understandings of social actors, in addition to the need to understand the conceptual and theoretical frameworks of our fellow scientists. Having adopted this perspective, this argument brings out some of the implications of our decisions to do so. But it does not show that this is the only way we can describe or explain the events we now refer to as "political phenomena," using the language of political actors. So long as we are clear about what we are doing, we are free to adopt a different perspective—to conceptualize our field as composed of muscle movements, if we like, or cybernetic processes, or whatever our imagination comes up with. So long as we do not fall into the trap of surreptitiously reintroducing the old vocabulary of action and drawing upon the explanatory power (or at least the familiarity) of this way of speaking, there is nothing in the ontological argument that can stop us.

Our notions of what there is, what kind of things constitute the world or, more narrowly, the political world, can hardly be divorced from our notion of how the world is to be explained. It is by now almost universally recognized that there is no way of showing that any particular categorial framework is uniquely correct, that it alone captures the true nature of reality and provides the appropriate place or pigeonhole for every possible phenomenon. Rather, we argue for the adequacy of a framework by showing that the theories and explanations it enables us to construct are enlightening, that they enable us to make sense out of a significant range of our experience. It is because of the explanatory power of these theories that we come to accept the existence of the entities posited by the theory, or its associated categorial framework. Thus, the ontological argument has things backwards, so to speak. It tries to restrict the ways we can explain things by reference to a theory of what there is, when its account of what there is could only be defended by exhibiting the way it enables us to explain our experience.

If the argument from ontology will not work, it at least suggests a more persuasive answer: We adopt the intentionalist position because we are interested in explaining events not under any description, but under their descriptions as human doings. I am not interested in why a person's arm goes up, but why someone votes for a particular candidate. I am not interested in "homeostatic equilibria of self-regulating systems," but in such things as "the orderly resolution of political and social conflict." Therefore I will not introduce concepts like the former unless they are firmly rooted in concepts like the latter. This appeal to our interests, then, does not preclude the development of concepts that go beyond the intentionalist perspective, but insists that such concepts not displace the intentionalist perspective.

But why should we have such interests? Why should we wish to constrain our knowledge-seeking activities in this way? To appeal to "interest" is woefully inadequate, unless one can give an account of these interests. And such an account, I think, must ultimately be a moral account. It must ultimately justify our interests in terms of basic and fundamental values. In this case I think the value involved is clear: It is the value of human emancipation. The promise of social science is to liberate us from the power of causal conditions that restrict the scope of our free, self-directed activity.

What I have in mind by this argument can best be clarified by returning for a moment to the discussion of how the need for theories arises directly from the interpretative paradigm itself. It arises not because interpretative explanations are somehow incomplete without the specification of a nomological state-ment, or because they are incapable of explaining social inter-action, but because they are incapable of explaining interaction in which the consequences of our behavior cannot be deter-mined by tracing them through their effects on the situations of particular individuals. These are situations that are, we might say, opaque to the individuals involved in them—opaque in the sense that, without a theoretical understanding of their situa-tion, they will be unable to direct their behavior in accordance with their own values and purposes. In this chapter I have discussed only those cases of opacity that are due to the complexity of the structure of interaction, but the range of such situations is much greater than this. To see this, consider the point I made above regarding the presupposition of ration-ality for intentionalist explanations. Such explanations, I argued, explain what someone does by showing how it can be seen to "make sense" in terms of the agent's beliefs, purposes, and situation. But "rationality" is a matter of degree. Very often we find that we can only more or less "make sense" of what someone does. People are not always clear to themselves about why they do what they do; they may be deeply ambivalent about some of their objectives, and they may be unable to acknowledge some of their own needs and values. Moreover, even if a person's behavior is intelligible given the person's goals and beliefs, these goals and beliefs may themselves be less than fully coherent. For example, the person may misunderstand the situation he or she is in and therefore act on the basis of false beliefs. In all of these cases we can say that the situation is opaque to the social actors involved, or even that they are opaque to themselves.

Such situations are inimical to human freedom in the sense that they prevent or make it impossible for people to be self-determining and to direct their actions in accordance with their own conscious goals. To the extent that they are ignorant of the possible effects of their actions, or to the extent that the reasons for their own behavior are unclear to themselves, they are unable to determine the conditions of their own lives and their powers of self-direction are limited. I might add that this is a very broad notion of freedom. But it is easy to see how such unclarity and ignorance can be part of the conditions that sustain structures of domination that restrict negative liberty as well. For it may be a condition of class rule in certain kinds of society that the members of that society be ignorant of the political mechanisms that determine the policy outputs of the government, or that they not acknowledge to themselves the ways in which certain aspects of their lives are demeaning, leading them to adopt an attitude of resignation rather than resistance.

A social science based on and developing out of the interpretative perspective holds out the possibility of liberating people from these kinds of conditions. It does so because it develops causal laws that enable us to explain patterns of interaction that otherwise would be opaque to them, and also to explain the conditions under which fully intentional action may be possible, that is, the conditions under which the assumption of rationality is warranted. By coming to an understanding of these laws, situations that were once opaque to social actors may no longer be so, and social actors may be able to determine conditions which once determined them. Because social laws, given the approach I have been advocating, develop out of a framework that is based upon the intentionalist perspective, they do not hold independently of the beliefs, values, and generally the self-understandings of social actors, and so it may be possible for these laws to be defeated, as it were, by the actors coming to change their self-understandings in light of their awareness of these laws. This, of course, marks a crucial difference between the natural sciences and social sciences which take an interpretative approach.

There is a sense in which all science is emancipatory, insofar as it gives us reliable laws that we can use in determining the consequences of our behavior and in providing us with the knowledge we need to establish control over natural or social processes. When we use scientific laws in this way, however, we do not "defeat" them so much as rely upon them in order to achieve a condition more to our liking. When we put fluoride in our drinking water, we are not defeating the law or lawlike statement linking the presence of fluoride to the absence of tooth decay, but we are using it. If we achieve our purpose, we will have added an additional piece of evidence to the data supporting the law, and explained by it. Of course, this may also be true of some social and political theories; when we use Keynesian theory to restore full employment, we are doing much the same thing as putting fluoride in our drinking water.

But that is not the only way that social laws may be practical, at least when they are formulated from an intentionalist perspective. For example, a hypothesis that is suggested by the Stanford study of the origins of World War I is that, as a crisis deepens, political elites will systematically misperceive the messages they receive from opposing elites and the messages they send to opposing elites, viewing the level of hostility expressed in the messages received as higher than it really is, and the level of hostility in their own messages as lower than it really is (Holsti, 1965; Holsti et al., 1968). If this is the case, it is easy to see how a crisis can lead to a war that no one intends and also, I might add, how the interpretative perspective is inadequate to explain the outcome by itself. When I first learned of the Stanford study in graduate school, I was told that its results were known to the American decision makers during the Cuban missile crisis and that they took pains to avoid misperceiving the messages that they were exchanging with the Russians. Consequently, the story continued, these perceptual distortions were not observed during this crisis.

I do not know whether this story is true, but it certainly could be. That is sufficient to illustrate the way in which a social law may be "defeated" rather than merely used. By becoming aware of the power that certain conditions have over us, we may acquire the power to master them and so to be free.

Another way of putting this point would be to say that a condition for certain social laws to hold may be that the participants in the social interaction be ignorant of the law in question. By discovering and communicating knowledge of such causal regularities to social actors, political and social inquiry may have a direct effect on the form of social interaction. To the extent that the occurrence of certain social processes depends upon the ignorance of the participants in those processes, the knowledge that results from political inquiry would cause those processes to be altered in potentially fundamental ways.

This concern with increasing the possible scope for human self-determination is of particular importance for political science, because the political has long been understood as that sphere of social life in which we might collectively and deliberately shape the conditions of our common life. One important dimension of this conception of politics is the concept of legislation, particularly the framing of the basic laws or constitution of a society. For in deliberately adopting certain rules, we decide to shape our lives in one way rather than another. Of course, this is not the only possible understanding of politics. It has also been viewed in essentially reductionist terms, and legislation might be seen less as deliberative action and more as the outcome of the blind interaction of social forces. Even those who envision the political as a sphere of human freedom recognize that this must be, in part, an ideal. One of the purposes of political inquiry, from this point of view, is to contribute to the realization of that ideal by providing the kind of knowledge necessary for people to be autonomous political actors. Ultimately, the goal of political science is to enlarge the area within which intentionalist explanations are possible by reducing to a minimum the sources of opacity in our collective life.

It will often be the case that knowledge by itself will not be sufficient, for most laws will not depend upon our self-understandings in such a simple way that by knowing the law, we would thereby acquire the power to defeat it. Generally, it will be necessary to use political knowledge to shape new institutions and practices if we are dissatisfied with existing forms of interaction. Moreover, some laws may express boundary conditions on possible forms of social or political organization, which rule out certain combinations of elements as nomically impossible. For example, it may be impossible to have a market economy, including a free labor market, and equality in income among adults. Of course, even such knowledge may be liberating, not because it may enable us to transform our situation, but because it enables us to know the limits within which such transformation is possible. And other laws might be applicable only in an instrumental or engineering manner, therefore giving differential power to those who have the necessary knowledge and resources to make use of them. Thus, while an intentionalist political science may not, in the end, fulfill the promise of emancipation, it at least offers the possibility of doing so, and that is all we can ask.

NOTES

1. Panel on "Business, Labor and the State in Industrial Democracies," American Political Science Association Annual Meeting, Washington, D.C., 1980.
2. Cited from the back cover of the paperback edition of Heclo (1974).
3. I have been discussing intentional explanations only in the context of accounting for specific actions. As I have argued elsewhere (Moon, 1975), such

explanations make reference to action descriptions and principles that are aspects of the practices and culture of a particular society, and that themselves require interpretation. Such interpretations are among the most important kinds of "theory" that we have in political science. In this chapter, however, I am considering theory only in the narrow sense in which theories involve interconnected sets of lawlike propositions.

REFERENCES

Davidson, D. (1970) "Mental events," pp. 79-101 In L. Foster and J. W. Swanson (eds.) *Experience and Theory.* London: Duckworth.

Downs, A. (1957) *An Economic Theory of Democracy.* New York: Harper & Row.

Elias, N. (1978) *What is Sociology?* London: Hutchinson.

Goldman, Alvin (1970) *A Theory of Human Action.* Englewood Cliffs, NJ: Prentice--Hall.

Greenstein, F. (1979-1980) "Eisenhower as an activist President." *Political Science Quarterly* 94 (Winter): 575-599.

Heclo, H. (1974) *Modern Social Politics in Britain and Sweden.* New Haven, CT: Yale University Press.

Holsti, O. (1965) "The 1914 case." *American Political Science Review* 59.

———, R. North, and R. Brody (1968) "Perception and action in the 1914 crisis," in J. David Singer (ed.) *Quantitative International Politics.* New York: Free Press.

Louch, A. (1969) *Explanation and Human Action.* Berkeley: University of California Press.

Marx, K. (1844) *Economic and Philosophical Manuscripts,* in T. B. Bottomore (ed.) *Early Writings.* New York: McGraw-Hill.

Moon, J. D. (1975) "The logic of political inquiry." in F. Greenstein and N. W. Polsby (eds.) *Handbook of Political Science* (Vol. 1). Reading, MA: Addison-Wesley.

Richardson, W. and A. Somit (1980) "Excellence and its recognition: the dissertation awards in political science." *Political Science* (Summer): 286-291.

Rosenberg, A. (1976) *Microeconomic Laws.* Pittsburgh: University of Pittsburgh Press.

von Wright, G. H. (1971) *Explanation and Understanding.* Ithaca, NY: Cornell University Press.

Winch, P. (1958) *The Idea of a Social Science.* London: Routledge & Kegan Paul.

7

The Three Worlds of Action

A Metatheoretical Synthesis of Institutional Approaches

LARRY L. KISER and ELINOR OSTROM

Studying the effects of institutional arrangements on patterns of human behavior and the resulting patterns of outcomes is a strategy of inquiry used by scholars straddling the academic disciplines of political science and economics. Institutional arrangements are the rules used by individuals for determining who and what are included in decision situations, how information is structured, what actions can be taken and in what sequence, and how individual actions will be aggregated into collective decisions. Institutional arrangements are thus complex composites of rules, all of which exist in a language shared by some community of individuals rather than as the physical parts of some external environment.

As language-based phenomena, institutional rules do not impinge directly on the world (V. Ostrom, 1980). A change in a decision rule (for example, adopting a two-thirds instead of a

AUTHORS' NOTE: Major portions of this manuscript were written while Kiser was a postdoctoral trainee at the Workshop in Political Theory and Policy Analysis at Indiana University, under an NIMH traineeship on "Research Training in Institutional Analysis and Design" (Grant 5 T32 MH15222). The chapter draws on a long tradition majority voting rule), cannot have an immediate and direct effect on some physical distribution of things. Institutional change impinges on the world by affecting the shared understandings of individuals making choices within decision situations affected by the rules. Effects in the world will result, if they do, in three steps. First, the individuals affected by a change in rules must be cognizant of and abide by the change. Second, institutional change has to affect the strategies they adopt. Third, the aggregation of changed individual strategies must lead to different results. Not all changes in behavior lead to changes in outcomes. A change in the institutional arrangement for deciding energy policy, for example, does not change patterns of energy use until individuals in their everyday lives lower thermostat settings, join a car pool, buy a solar heater, and so on.

This complex set of transformations from rules through common understanding of decision situations to individual behavior is difficult to analyze and understand. The purpose of this chapter is to provide a metatheoretical framework for understanding the complex set of transformations that link institutional arrangements to individual behavior and aggregate results occurring in the "real" world. The framework is *meta*theoretical, because it describes the array of elements that are used in specific theories about institutions rather than presenting a particular theory.

This metatheoretical framework focuses on the scholarly work in political science and economics that uses a microinstitutional approach to the analysis of political phenomena. The microinstitutional approach is "micro" because it starts

---

of work and discussion at the workshop and could not have been written without the extended discussions and comments on earlier, related manuscripts among participants including Deby Dean, Vernon Greene, John Hamilton, Roger B. Parks, Stephen L. Percy, Ron Oakerson, Vincent Ostrom, Rick Wilson, and Susan Wynne. We appreciate the helpful comments we received on the first draft of this manuscript from David Austin, Judy Gillespie, David Kessler, Roger B. Parks, Cyrus Reed, and Rick Wilson. We also appreciate Teresa Therrien's careful work in editing and typing this manuscript.

from the individual as a basic unit of analysis to explain and predict individual behavior and resulting aggregated outcomes. It is an "institutional" approach because major explanatory variables include the set of institutional arrangements that individuals use to affect the incentive systems of a social order and the impact of incentive systems on human behavior.

Patterns of human action and the results that occur in interdependent choice-making situations are the phenomena to be explained using this approach. Interdependence occurs whenever results are dependent on the actions of more than one individual. Interdependence can at times produce aggregated results that vary dramatically from individual expectations or preferences. Interdependence describes hundreds of everyday experiences as individuals interact with one another, trying to achieve a better life in the marketplace, within families, in clubs, in neighborhoods, in legislatures, in bureaucracies, and in other collective arrangements (see Schelling, 1978, for a discussion of such situations).

Interdependent decision situations can be incredibly complex. Institutional analysts abstract from this complexity by modeling typical decision situations and the behavior of individuals involved in such situations. Analysts attempt to identify the smallest set of working parts to yield a coherent and testable theory for observed patterns of actions and results. Given the complexity of the theoretical models used in institutional analysis, social scientists wishing to understand this literature are frequently confused about how the various elements of the theories are linked together and about how theorists use key terms. We try to provide a synthesis and overview of the political-economy literature that uses the individual as a unit of analysis while asking how institutional arrangements affect the level, type, and distribution of outcomes. This chapter is like a schematic road map to a complex, difficult, and changeable academic terrain. We hope it will help the neophyte interested in gaining an overview before approaching the specifics. We also hope it will help those who have traveled the hills and valleys of institutional analysis and who may wish to step back with us and look at the slippery terrain they have traveled from a more general perspective.

While many authors have contributed to this approach, we have been particularly influenced in offering this synthesis by the work of Kenneth Arrow, James Buchanan, John R. Commons, Anthony Downs, Frank Knight, Mancur Olson, Vincent Ostrom, William Riker, Kenneth Shepsle, Herbert Simon, Thomas Schelling, Gordon Tullock, and Oliver Williamson. Instead of peppering this essay with extensive and disruptive citations, we have provided the reader with a general bibliography of many of the key articles and books related to the synthesis presented here.

THE THEORETICAL WORKING PARTS
OF INSTITUTIONAL ANALYSIS

Implicit or explicit in the theories explaining individual behavior within institutional structures are five working parts, including (1) the decision maker, (2) the community affected by interdependent decision-making, (3) events (or goods and services) that interacting individuals seek to produce and consume, (4) institutional arrangements guiding individual decisions, and (5) the decision situation in which individuals make choices. Political economists select appropriate assumptions about the attributes of each working part. The set of assumptions about the working parts explains actions by individual decision makers and aggregated outcomes. Figure 7.1 shows the relationship among the five working parts, actions, and outcomes.

The framework displayed in Figure 7.1 rests on a methodological individualist perspective. Attributes of the individual decision maker constitute the core of the analysis. Assumptions about the individual animate all particular models based on this microinstitutional frame (Popper, 1967; Simon, 1978). However, several alternative assumptions may be made within the model of the individual used by a particular theorist. This approach is distinct from macroinstitutional political economy which animates theoretical models with social forces beyond the influence of individuals. Individuals in macroinstitutional political economy have little choice but to obey these over-riding social forces.

While methodological individualism places the attributes of individual decision makers at the core of the analytical frame-work, the other working parts are equally important to the explanations derived from the framework. The other working parts establish the environment in which individuals make choices. Combining assumptions about all five working parts enables political economists to predict two types of results. One prediction addresses individual decision makers' strategies or actions, and the second prediction addresses the aggregation of individual actions into outcomes for the community.

Political economists rarely develop all five working parts within a given analysis. Writers tend to focus, instead, on changes within one or two working parts, assuming that all other working parts remain unchanged. Unfortunately, such assumptions are often implicit and lead to error. Holding other factors constant is not equivalent to ignoring them. The con-figuration of working parts constitutes the environment in which individuals make choices; thus, analysis must recognize the condition of the unchanging factors (see Boynton, Chapter 2 in this volume). Ignoring any of the working parts can misrepresent the decision maker's environment and produce misleading predictions.

To use an analogy, one can think of a specific model devel-oped to explain the effect of institutional arrangements as a large tinkertoy composed of at least five components, each of which also contains a number of elements or subcomponents. The large tinkertoy model is built to resemble a more complex and indeterminate machine that operates in the real world. The tinkertoy is a successful model for some purpose if it helps predict what the complex machine will do under particular circumstances. No single tinkertoy model is used to predict the actions for all complex machines that might be modeled by institutional theorists. As different machines are modeled, major changes may be made in some subcomponents, while other working parts may remain relatively stable. However, changes in some of the working parts may require changes in others, since considerable interdependence exists among the particular assumptions made about different working parts.

Political economists apply the working parts of microinstitutional analysis at three related but distinct levels of analysis. One is the *operational level*, which explains the world of action. The second is the *collective choice level*, which explains the world of authoritative decision-making. The third is the *constitutional level*, which explains the design of collective choice mechanisms. The operational, collective choice, and constitutional levels of analysis are the "three worlds" referred to in our title. Figure 7.2, which appears later in this chapter, displays the three levels of analysis and the components of each level. It shows that the same working parts make up all three worlds. This chapter, therefore, concentrates first on each of the working parts, applying them to the world of action. We then apply the working parts to the other two levels of analysis.

Attributes of the Individual

Microinstitutional political economy emphasizes that only individuals, not groups, act. To predict that action, theorists must at least make assumptions about

(1) the individual's level of information about the decision situation,
(2) the individual's valuation of potential outcomes and of alternative actions possible within the decision situation, and
(3) the individual's calculation process for selecting among alternative actions or strategies.

Individuals act to achieve valued outcomes; therefore, individuals must have some notion of how actions link up with outcomes and how values are realized by selecting among alternative actions.

Neoclassical economists handle the three minimum assumptions by modeling an individual producer in a competitive market as having perfect information about relevant goods and resource prices, as valuing only profits, and as calculating to maximize expected profits. Herbert Simon and others influenced by him (see Williamson, 1975) develop alternative models by assuming that the individual producer possesses incomplete information about the decision situation. These political economists also assume that individuals value multiple outcomes rather than just profits and that individuals sometimes have difficulty discriminating among the rankings of these outcomes. The producer is much less precise in decision-making than the producer in the neoclassical model, searching for information and learning the characteristics of the decision situation. The Simon-type producer is less apt than the neoclassical producer to maximize values and is more likely to seek satisficing levels.

The individual in both the neoclassical and the Simon approaches is rational, although scholars within the neoclassical tradition frequently criticize Simon's work as "antirational." Simon (1957, 1972, 1978) defends his model of the individual as intendedly rational. The difference between the two specific models is the amount of information that individuals possess about themselves and their environment. The difference causes the individual to use a different calculating process for deciding how to act within a given decision situation.

Specific assumptions about information, valuation, and calculation in the model of the individual help to shape the overall model of interdependent choice. Neoclassical assumptions of complete information and profit maximization yield, when combined with the other working parts, a highly determinate, machinelike general theory. Assumptions of incomplete information, multiple values, and satisficing yield a less determinate, more flexible theory of choice (see V. Ostrom and Hennessey, 1975; V. Ostrom, 1976). The neoclassical assumptions are useful when modeling uncomplicated market exchange situations, but Simon-type assumptions are apt to be more useful

when modeling more complex situations where options continually shift.

Attributes of the Decision Situation

Figure 7.1 shows that the attributes of the individuals combine with the attributes of the decision situation to yield
individuals' actions or strategies. The decision maker, in other
words, chooses a strategy that is suitable to the decision situation. An individual with given attributes will make different
choices as decision situations change. Also, as noted earlier,
changes in the attributes of decision situations can require
changes in the attributes of the individual decision maker.
Particular assumptions about the individual's valuation of outcomes and calculation process must be compatible with the
decision situation.

The literature on game theory investigates the attributes of
decision situations, developing attributes such as

(1) the number of decision makers involved;
(2) the types of choices available to the decision maker;
(3) the linkages between actions and results;
(4) complexity;
(5) repetiveness;
(6) types of outcomes (zero-sum, positive sum, and so on);
(7) durability, stability, reversibility, and vulnerability to threat of
     outcomes; and
(8) possibilities for communication among interacting decision makers.

Decision theorists who are not interested in the study of
institutional arrangements stop with a model of the decision
situation. Most game theorists, for example, do not inquire
about the variables that affect a decision situation. The decision
situation is itself taken as a given rather than as the result of
other variables. Considerable theoretical advances in decision
theory have been based on an in-depth examination of the
behavior of differently modeled individuals in differently structured decision situations. Mancur Olson (1965), for example,

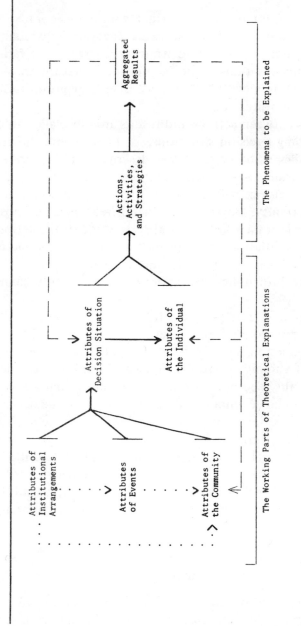

Figure 7.1 The Working Parts of Institutional Analysis

develops the concept of the free rider within the context of alternative decision situations, showing that an individual is more apt to choose a free-riding strategy in large-group rather than small-group situations. Other writers note that the tragedy of the commons is more likely to occur in large-group rather than in small-group situations.

The linkages between actions and results are especially important in describing decision situations, as this is where the concept of the degree of certainty is described. To describe a situation as certain is to assert that each alternative action available to a decision maker links to one and only one result. Risk and uncertainty, on the other hand, recognize the possibility of multiple results linked to at least some of the actions. Risk describes a situation where probability distributions across alternative results can be known, while uncertainty describes a situation where probability distributions across results cannot be known.

This chapter does not permit a full review of the attributes for decision situations. Hamburger (1979) presents an elementary introduction to this literature, outlining alternative descriptions of gaming situations and developing the relationship between the decision situation, the individual decision maker, and the choice among strategies. In general, the decision situation describes the array of choices confronting the decision maker and the pattern of consequences likely to flow from alternative choices. The attributes of the individual describe the capabilities and motives of the individual in the decision situation. The mix of the decision situation's attributes and the individual's attributes causes the individual to select particular actions.

Actions and Strategies

Microinstitutional political economy predicts individuals' actions and strategies and aggregated results flowing from models of decision makers within defined decision situations. An action in tennis, for example, can be either charging the net or defending the baseline. The player's choice depends on the player and the situation.

Political economists distinguish between actions and strategies. An action is like a "move" in a game, while a strategy is a sequence of moves. Thus, situations permitting only a single act at a particular decision point prohibit strategy, while repetitive situations encourage it. The decision maker in repetitive situations may make the same move every time the decision situation repeats, or the decision maker may randomly switch from one move to another. The consistent approach is called a "pure" strategy and the switching approach a "mixed" strategy.

Strategy implies commitment to a method for selecting actions over time. A strategy is a plan of action, often contingent upon other decision makers' actions. The strategy of "tit for tat" in extended Prisoners' Dilemma games is a contingent strategy. One player cooperates on the second play of the game, if the other player cooperates on the first play of game. Complex decision situations such as those in chess require contingent strategy, because a player can select the best move only after the opposing player makes a move.

Strategy also involves activities such as information gathering, giving, and withholding. Also, strategies include threats, guile, bargaining, and force. Some strategies are "sophisticated" plans where an individual makes real or apparent sacrifices on initial rounds of a decision situation to increase the possibility for gains in later rounds. Farquharson (1969) discusses the strategy of voting for a less favored option early in a contest to increase the probability of being able to vote for a more favored option later. Another sophisticated plan is the act of binding oneself irrevocably to particular future actions. Individuals often precommit when they fear they will succumb to short-run temptations that counter long-run interests (Elster, 1979; Thaler and Sheffrin, 1981).

Aggregated Results

The mathematical transformation of individual acts into group results often surprises the people whose acts produced the results. Individuals sometimes do not connect aggregate results with their own individual actions. Thomas Schelling (1978) gives an example of aggregation in the children's game of musical chairs, where every child rushes to sit in a chair when the music stops. The result is that one child is always left standing. Regardless of how determined each child is to sit and how aggressively each child plays the game, the mathematical transformation of the actions to results is always the same. There is always one more child in the game than there are chairs; therefore, someone must stand.

The result in musical chairs is intended, but the results in many group situations are unintended. Schelling gives another example: individual drivers slowing down to look at a rush-hour automobile accident in the opposite lane of an expressway. Drivers would be happy with a quick, ten-second look; but the resulting traffic jam gives them an extra ten-minute drive home. Each driver acts to participate, at least vicariously, in the excitement of the accident; but the result is boredom. When complaining about the traffic jam later, many drivers probably fail to admit that their own actions helped to produce their misery. Thomas Hobbes, writing long before the age of the automobile, recognized the problem when he described men in the state of nature striving for their own good and finding only misery.

Why do individuals take actions that bring on misery? How can they avoid the misery and realize happiness instead? These kinds of questions lead us to focus on the left side of Figure 7.1, to examine attributes of institutional arrangements, attributes of events, and attributes of community as they affect decision situations.

Institutional Arrangements

Economists and political scientists rejected for sometime any self-conscious study of institutional arrangements. Both disciplines placed these "skeletons" in the academic closet for many years.[1] Only recently has work on institutional arrangements reappeared in respectable academic journals and publishing houses (Blumstein, 1981; Riker, 1980; and Shepsle, 1979). The relatively recent attention to institutions means that the conception of institutional arrangements is necessarily incomplete. To streamline work in this area and to encourage additional analysis, we propose a new conceptualization of institutional arrangements. Our purpose is to develop a typology that can be applied to a wide range of institutional conditions.

Institutional arrangements are the sets of rules governing the number of decision makers, allowable actions and strategies, authorized results, transformations internal to decision situations, and linkages among decision situations. Examining institutional arrangements involves a stepping back in the process to look at one of the three major factors affecting the structure of decision situations. The givens are no longer givens but rather the results of the interaction of rules, events, and community.

Hurwicz (1973) uses the term "decision mechanism" to describe institutional arrangements, conveying the image of a device constraining and guiding the choices that individuals make. Institutional arrangements simultaneously restrict and expand the freedom for individual action. As John R. Commons (1950: 21) wrote, "an institution is collective action in control, liberation, and expansion of individual action" (see also Knight, 1965: 304). Persons interacting in a market situation are restricted, because they can only conduct particular types of voluntary transactions. Persons in legislative situations are also restricted, because they can vote only on amendments and legislation according to highly formalized procedures.

But institutional rules also expand freedom by increasing predictability in decision situations. Decision makers knowing that rules restrict actions by other decision makers can predict responses to their own actions better than they could without those rules. An auto salesperson, for example, is freer to grant credit to a buyer, knowing that rules require future payment and that courts exist to enforce those rules. Otherwise, buyers and sellers would limit themselves to transactions with immediate payment in full.

Rules, of course, require enforcement to be effective; but much theoretical work overlooks the enforcement aspect by assuming that decision makers take only lawful actions. The assumption simplifies analysis, enabling analysts to concentrate on issues unrelated to enforcement. But if the assumption is unconscious, the analysis can yield implications incongruent with a real world of illegal behavior. Sometimes analysis needs to include enforcement variables to explain real-world actions. Interaction with complicated games like football is more predictable when on-site referees aggressively mete out penalties to keep play within the rules.

This does not imply that enforcement is the only reason that individuals follow rules.[2] People also follow rules because those in a community share a belief that the rules are fair. Individuals within such a community, expecting others to follow the rules, see opportunities to pursue their own interests by following the rules too. Without this shared belief, enforcement would become too expensive to maintain regularity and predictability in ongoing human relationships.

Institutional arrangements transform an individual's actions into outcomes affecting both the actor and others. Predictability of action-outcome linkages, therefore, depends upon both transformations in the physical world and transformations within decision mechanisms in the institutional world. A person drives safely to work because the physical operation of cars on the road is predictable and because other motorists' behavior according to traffic rules is predictable. The driver's control over outcomes increases because each motorist possesses rights of way on the road and commensurate duties to observe equivalent rights of others.

Scholars frequently refer to institutional arrangements by organization names such as markets, legislatures, courts, private firms, public bureaus, families, contracts, and international treaties. But we propose a more abstract reference that facilitates comparison among organizational structures. The proposal looks to the rules that characterize all institutional arrangements—rules delineating the participants and allowable actions, rules distributing authority among participants, rules aggregating participants' choices into collective decisions, rules outlining procedure and information flows, and rules distributing payoffs among participants. These rules may be formal, that is, detailed and written, or informal, that is, simply understood by participants in the arrangement. Informal rules are what Commons (1959: 138) calls the "working rules of a going concern," rules that evolve perhaps unconsciously with the functioning of the organization.

We distinguish between institutional arrangements and organizations. Political economists frequently interchange the terms, but in our attempt to abstract comparisons among organizations we define institutional arrangements as distinct from organizations. We define organizations as composites of participants following rules governing activities and transactions to realize particular outputs. These activities occur within specific facilities. The rules, which are components of all organizations, are the institutional arrangements.

The distinction between institutional arrangements and organizations avoids problems of classifying organizations by proper name. National legislatures, for example, make up a single class; but legislatures can function very differently from one another. Identifying the rules or the institutional arrangements of the legislatures helps one to understand those important differences, whereas classifying by the term "legislature" obscures vital information about the way those organizations operate (see Shepsle, 1979).

Our typology of institutional rules classifies rules according to their effect on decision situations and on individual choice behavior within decision situations.[3] The typology concentrates on (1) the entry and exit conditions for participating in organizations, (2) allowable actions and allowable outcomes from interaction within organizations, (3) the distribution of authority among positions within organizations to take particular

actions, (4) the aggregation of joint decisions within organizations, (5) procedural rules in complex situations linking
decision situations together, and (6) information constraints
within organizations.

The types of rules that address each of these six issues are (1)
boundary rules, (2) scope rules, (3) position and authority rules,
(4) aggregation rules, (5) procedural rules, and (6) information
rules. Each set of rules help to shape incentives facing individuals within decision situations. Other aspects of institutional
arrangements may also affect decision makers' incentives, but
we think these six include aspects theorists identify as most
important to explain behavior within and outcomes from interdependent decision situations.

The rules in intercollegiate tennis provide an example of
institutional arrangements. The rules delineate

(1) who can enter tennis as a competitive sport within the member
    universities and the conditions under which players lose eligibility
    (boundary rules);
(2) the size of the court, the height of the net, the physical actions
    that a player is allowed to take, the number of times the ball can
    bounce on each side of the net, and the allowed set of outcomes
    (scope rules);
(3) the rights and duties assigned to players and to referees (position
    and authority rules);
(4) how specific acts and physical results are scored and aggregated
    into wins and losses (aggregation rules);
(5) how players will proceed through tournament competition (pro-
    cedural rules); and
(6) how information about opponents' strategies, tournament rules,
    specific calls, and other matters are conveyed to participants
    (information rules).

Any particular model of an institutional arrangement will
need to make particular assumptions about boundary rules,
scope rules, position and authority rules, aggregation rules,
procedure rules, and information rules. Given the large number
of combinations of specific rules that can be designed, we are

unlikely ever to have a complete theory of institutions.[4] However, substantial theoretical and empirical work has recently focused on the effect of one or more of these types of rules or the behavior of individuals in particular types of decision situations.

The Attributes of Events

People have long been aware that the nature of goods affects calculations bearing upon human welfare. Aristotle (1962: 58), for example, observed, "that which is common to the greatest number has the least care bestowed upon it." This aspect of decision-making has attracted even more attention with the growth of public-goods analysis in recent times.

The variety in goods and events is vast. But most of the variety is inconsequential to the effects of institutional arrangements on the results of human interaction. A given institutional arrangement can effectively guide resource allocation toward notably dissimilar goods. Arrangements within competitive markets, for example, effectively make both wheat and television sets available to consumers. But competitive markets are ineffective in making police protection or environmental clean-up available.

This section focuses on attributes of goods that distinguish wheat and television sets from police protection and environmental clean-up and that affect the ability of markets to make those goods available. The discussion identifies attributes of goods and events that help to shape individuals' decision-making incentives. The attributes include jointness of use, exclusion, degree of choice, and measurability.[5]

Jointness of Use or Consumption

Howard Bowen (1943-1944) distinguished between goods consumed simultaneously by more than one individual (joint consumption) and goods consumed by a single individual (separable consumption). The distinction is the effect that use by one individual has on the goods' availability to others. An individual's use of separable consumption goods reduces the goods' availability to others, while an individual's use of joint consumption goods permits simultaneous use by others. Paul Samuelson (1954, 1955) repeated this distinction a decade later with the classic series of articles on pure public goods. Samuelson called joint consumption goods public goods, defining "a public good as a good which is subject to joint or collective consumption where any one individual's consumption is *nonsubstractible* from any other individual's consumption of a good" (1954: 387; our emphasis). Samuelson (1954: 877) also noted that "a public consumption good differs from a private consumption good in that each man's consumption of it is related to the total by a condition of equality rather than that of summation."

Few, if any, joint consumption goods are perfectly nonsubtractible. The gravitational pull of the earth is an example: Regardless of the number of people using gravitational pull, the force is equally available to additional users. Most joint consumption goods are only partially nonsubtractible. When the number of users reaches some critical point, one person's use partially reduces the good's availability for simultaneous use by others. Highway congestion is an example. The highway is available for simultaneous use by many motorists, but as traffic builds during rush hours, one motorist's use of the highway causes delays and inconvenience for others. Buchanan (1970) identified the effects of congestion in public goods as erosion, noting the role of supply in contending against the degradation of public goods.

Exclusion

Scholars have extended the analysis of public goods, adding other characteristics to distinguish public from private goods. Musgrave (1959), Head (1962), and Olson (1965) identified the attribute of exclusion, noting that a public good makes excluding additional consumers infeasible once the good is available to any consumer. A private good, on the other hand, makes exclusion feasible. An individual can use the good without sharing it with other consumers. Anyone can benefit from a nonexcludable public good or event so long as nature or producers supply it. Nature supplies the air we breathe, and it is freely available to all. Producers supply views of buildings, and the views (whether obnoxious or enjoyable) are also freely available to all.

Both exclusion and jointness of consumption vary continuously. Goods are rarely totally excludable or totally nonexcludable, and they are rarely totally subtractible or totally nonsubtractible. But analysis frequently presumes pure categories to sharpen the distinction between public and private goods.

Exclusion and jointness of consumption are independent attributes, permitting a classification of goods according to Table 7.1. The table shows jointness of consumption with two columns, one for highly subtractible goods and one for less subtractible goods. The table shows exclusion with two rows, one for low-cost exclusion goods and one for high-cost exclusion goods. The result is four cells distinguishing private goods, which are highly subtractible and where exclusion is inexpensive, from public goods, which are less subtractible and where exclusion is expensive. Toll goods and common-pool resources range between these two extremes with both types possessing some attributes of publicness. Toll goods are less subtractible, but exclusion is cheap. Common-pool resources are highly subtractible, but exclusion is expensive.

Measurement

Since public goods are difficult to package or unitize, they are usually also difficult to measure. Measures such as hectares, meters, and kilograms do not apply. While other kinds of indexes are possible, such as decibels, degrees, and parts per million, aggregation is difficult with these measures. Sometimes indexes do not even exist. Thus, producers often know only imprecisely what they are producing, and consumers know only imprecisely what they are consuming. Cost calculations, valuation, and pricing are, therefore, often crude.

Private goods, on the other hand, are easier to package or unitize and, thus, to measure. This helps both producers and

TABLE 7.1   Jointness of Consumption

Exclusion	Highly Subtractible	Less Subractible
Exclusion		
Low cost	Private goods: bread, milk, automobiles, haircuts.	Toll goods: theaters, night clubs, telephone service, cable TV, electric power, library.
High cost	Common-pool resources: water pumped from a ground water basin, fish taken from an ocean, crede oil extracted from an oil pool	Public goods: peace and security, of a community, national defense, mosquito abatement, air pollution control, weather forecasts.

NOTE: Table 7.1 is adapted from V. Ostrom and E. Ostrom (1977a: 12).

consumers make more informed decisions regarding such goods. Producers apply more precise cost-accounting procedures and management controls when producing private goods, and consumers make more precise budgeting decisions when consuming private goods.

Degree of Choice

Nonsubtractible and nonexcludable goods frequently give individuals little choice about consumption. The mere existence of a commodity may force individuals to consume it or at least pay much to avoid consuming the commodity. Some forced consumers may not even value the commodity. Congested streets, for example, inconvenience local residents and shoppers, who are required to cope with the traffic whether they like it or not. Private goods, however, do not pose this problem. The individual who does not value a private good simply need not purchase it.

Institutional Arrangements and Public Goods

The capacity of individuals to achieve a relatively optimal level of any type of goods is dependent upon the type of institutional rules developed to relate individuals to one another and to events in the world. However, the design of effective institutional arrangements to produce public goods is more difficult than the design of effective institutional arrangements to produce private goods. Mancur Olson (1965) demonstrates that nonsubtractible and nonexcludable public goods present serious problems in human organization. Once a public good is supplied, all individuals within the relevant domain are free to use the good without paying toward the cost of producing it. Cost-minimizing individuals have an incentive to become "free riders," holding out on others who pay. The free riders' success encourages others to stop payment, too, causing a drop in the amount of the good supplied. Unless institutional changes create new incentives, each person responding to self-interest ignores the interests of others, and ultimately all suffer.

Economists have developed the implications of the public-private goods distinction for the market system, concluding that competitive markets fail to allocate resources toward public goods efficiently. In some cases the failure may be complete, with no production and consumption of the public good resulting. Welfare is maximized where the sum of all consumers' marginal rates of substitution (that is, valuation of marginal consumption units) equals the social marginal cost of producing the good. Voluntary market transactions fail to achieve this condition. The market distribution of prices for a public good among consumers is unlikely to correspond to the distribution of consumer marginal valuations, because markets generally require the same price from all consumers.

This problem does not develop in a market for private goods. Each consumer independently purchases more or less of the good at the market price, depending on consumer preferences. Consumers with marginal valuations exceeding the price of the good purchase additional units until marginal values fall to equal the price. Consumers with marginal valuations below the price reduce purchases until marginal values rise to equal the price. The result is that while consumers with different preferences pay the same price, the market permits efficient adjustment among consumers. Furthermore, competition among producers assures that producers use economically efficient means for producing the good.

Public-good situations usually require some form of collective action with sanctions compelling each individual to share in the production costs. Individuals in small groups can monitor each other's costs. Individuals in small groups can monitor each other's actions and personally coerce each other to share costs. Thus, families can effectively provide joint consumption goods for members. But large groups are not so effective with casual arrangements. Each individual is more anonymous, and each individual's share of the good seems insignificant. Thus, each is tempted to free-ride on payments by others, unless the group coerces payment from users. The lack of coercion leads to Aristotle's contention that the good or property shared by "the greatest number has the least care bestowed upon it."

Institutional arrangements with coercive sanctions are not sufficient to guarantee optimal amounts of public goods. Instruments of coercion may harm as well as help. As governmental institutions permit officials to deprive some citizens and reward others, institutional arrangements designed to advance the common good might become an instrument of tyranny instead. Moreover, difficulties in measuring the output of public goods and services imply that government officials have difficulties monitoring the performance of public employees. Service delivery, therefore, departs from desired levels.

Where citizens have little choice about the quality of public services supplied to them, they also have little incentive to do anything about those services. Citizens' costs of trying to change the quality can exceed increased benefits that individual citizens can expect. The structure of institutional arrangements may have some effect on the degree of choice that individuals have. Different electoral systems, such as the plurality-vote or single-member constituencies used in the United States, give more voice to individual constituents than other systems, such as the proportional-representation, party-list arrangements characteristic of Western Europe. Councilpersons representing local wards would be more sensitive to protests by local residents about how streets are used in those wards than are councilpersons elected at large. Voucher systems where individuals use a pro rata share of tax funds to obtain services from alternative vendors of educational services, for example, may allow for a much greater degree of choice on the part of individual users.

Our tennis example illustrates the influence of the attributes of goods, attributes on decision situations. Tennis players and spectators jointly consume the benefits of a game, but exclusion is relatively easy. Fencing tennis courts is legally allowable and is inexpensive. The fence helps to exclude individuals who do not qualify, by membership in a group or by admission price, for entry to the game. Thus, tennis is a toll good, fitting the northeast cell in Table 7.1. Private voluntary arrangements and collective arrangements both effectively make this good available to consumers.

Fencing also affects players' strategies during a game. A fence retains the ball, causing players to play more aggressively than they would without the fence. Aggressive play does not interfere with games in neighboring courts or require time out to chase an errant ball.

The Community

The community is the third cluster of variables constituting the decision situation. The community includes all individuals directly or indirectly affected by the decision situation. The attributes of the community relevant to institutional analysis include the level of common understanding, similarity in individuals' preferences, and the distribution of resources among those affected by a decision situation.

The relevant community in our tennis example includes the players and others affected by the game results, particularly by a continued iteration of the tennis games. In intercollegiate tennis, the community includes players, referees, judges, spectators, students, parents, and alumni. College administrators who govern student activities and who participate in inter-collegiate athletic associations are also part of the community. In intramural tennis the community is much smaller, often including only the opposing players. The differences in the community between intercollegiate and intramural tennis alter the competition and change decision situations for players. A player will probably use a strategy in an intercollegiate game that differs from his or her strategy in a friendly intramural game.

Level of Common Understanding

Common understanding among community members is necessary for interdependent decision situations. Without common understanding a community of individuals dissolves into a disorganized aggregate with no social cohesion. Common understanding among community members may grow from a history of shared experience, enhanced by common terms and resulting in common expectations.

Individuals cannot play a game without coming to a common understanding of the rules. Players must share a similar view of the range of allowable actions, or the distribution of rights and duties among players, of likely consequences, and of prefer-ences among players for alternative outcomes. Common under-standing, however, does not imply equal distribution of infor-mation among community members. Some common knowledge of the institutional constraints is necessary for interdependent decision-making, but participants may vary in their level of knowledge. Incentives, therefore, may differ among individuals (even individuals with similar preferences) choosing within similar decision situations.

Rule-ordered transformations do not, however, provide the level of predictability that physical mechanisms can provide. Part of the ambiguity arises from problems with human lan-guage. Montias (1976: 18) defines a rule as "a message stipulat-ing and constraining the actions of a set of participants for an indefinite period and under specified states of these individuals' environments." The messages, relying on language, are sometimes garbled or ambiguous. Because words are "symbols that name, and thus, stand for classes of things and relationships" (V. Ostrom, 1980: 10), words are always simpler than the phenomena to which they refer.

Stability in rule-ordered transformations depends upon shared definitions of the words formulating the rules. Even if all community members conscientiously try to implement a confusing law, it will yield irregular behavior when individuals interpret the law in a variety of circumstances. As "rules are not self-formulating, self-determining, or self-enforcing" (V. Ostrom, 1980: 11), individuals must formulate the rules, apply them to particular circumstances, and enforce performance consistent with them. Ambiguity can arise at any of these points.

Changing circumstances aggravate the instability in rule-ordered transformations. Vincent Ostrom (1980: 1) writes,

> the exigencies to which rules apply are themselves subject to change. Applying language to changing configurations of development increases the ambiguities and threatens the shared criteria of choice with erosion of their appropriate meaning.

Predicting behavior, therefore, on the basis of rules is necessarily imprecise, with the degree of imprecision depending on the existence of mechanisms for resolving conflicting interpretations of rules. Such mechanisms enhance the shared meaning of rules and reduce variation in behavior.

When individuals frequently interact directly with one another in a particular decision situation, as in tennis, the level of common understanding is higher than when individuals participate infrequently and in widely disparate locations. However, a geographically dispersed community can interact in a market when its members share a common understanding of the market's structure through frequent interaction and through enforcement of property law.

Level of Common Agreement
About Values

A second community characteristic affecting the decision situation is the level of agreement among members when evaluating actions and results in interdependent decision-making. This is especially important in situations that force consumption upon individuals in a community. Lack of agreement usually distorts the distribution of cost among community members, causing ferment among those assuming disproportionate burdens. This helps to explain the general unrest within the United States during the war in Vietnam, which forced many citizens to participate in what they considered to be an immoral war. Common agreement about values is less important in situations involving private goods.

Community agreement about institutional arrangements, however, is always important. Agreement about the moral correctness and the fairness of rules constraining decision-making reduces the need for enforcement. Otherwise, individuals seek to evade and change the rules. Individuals' actions become less predictable and the order of the system breaks down, causing authorities to invest heavily to monitor community members' actions and to impose sanctions on members taking unauthorized actions.

Distribution of Resources

A third attribute of the community relevant to institutional analysis is the resource distribution among community members. A competitive market is defined to be a situation of nearly equal distribution among producers. No single producer possesses enough resources to manipulate market prices or to influence market transactions.

Individuals controlling disproportionate resource shares for participating in particular decision structures fundamentally affect the nature of the decision situation. The decision situation differs from the equal distribution case, even when institutional rules and attributes of events remain the same. Thus, if a few firms gain market control, the situation changes from one involving many decision makers (a competitive situation) to one involving a few (an oligopolistic situation). Economic theory predicts that producer decisions in a competitive situation will differ from decisions in an oligopoly. Decisions in legislatures and other political organizations also change when power distributions, say from leadership qualities, grow less equal.

FEEDBACK AMONG THE WORKING PARTS

The discussion so far addresses only the rightward flow of relationships among the working parts. Figure 7.1 shows that institutional arrangements, attributes of goods and events, and attributes of community combine to determine attributes of the decision situation. The attributes of the decision situation combine with the attributes of the individual decision maker to yield actions and strategies. Actions and strategies aggregate finally into results or outcomes.

Figure 7.1, however, also shows feedback relationships moving from right to left. Aggregated results subsequently affect the community attributes, attributes of the decision situation, and attributes of the individual. Reasoning along the feedback paths presumes that the working parts of the framework have cycled at least once, with individuals choosing in a given decision situation, acting on those choices, and realizing outcomes. The feedbacks show the dynamic quality of the framework.

Consider the feedback from results to the attribute of the community. Perhaps the most direct effect of outcomes is to increase the community's shared experience from interaction. This alters the community and decisions by members of the community. Our tennis example illustrates the change. If a player decides during a particular volley to charge the net, both players experience the result. The next time the opportunity to charge the net arises, even though the physical situation is exactly like the first occasion, the decision situation is not the same. The opposing player has some insight into the first player's strategy and ability and has some insight into his or her own ability to counter the charge to the net. The links between alternative actions and their consequences, therefore, change, perhaps causing the offensive player this time to play toward the baseline.

Feedback from results to the attributes of the individual shows the effects of experience on the individual decision maker rather than on the community. Whereas feedback to the community alters subsequent decision situations, feedback to the individual alters the decision maker's understanding of the decision situation. The decision maker, therefore, may change strategies in the situation, and may even change objectives.

The tennis player having charged the net during an earlier volley and scored, and may decide that scoring is not as enjoyable as expected, if the tactic demoralizes the opposing player. The game ceases to be fun, so the next time the player may change strategy by challenging the opposing player with a returnable volley.

THE THREE LEVELS OF ANALYSIS

The analytic components of the world of action discussed above apply to all three levels of analysis. Figure 7.2 shows the constitutional choice, collective choice, and operational levels of analysis and shows the same working parts in each level. Each section of the diagram includes attributes of institutional arrangements, events, community, the decision situation, and the individual decision maker. Each section also includes either symbolic or real action and aggregated results.

The World of Action

The first level of analysis is the world of action or the operational level, shown at the extreme right of the figure. Individuals functioning at this level either take direct action or adopt a strategy for future actions, depending on expected

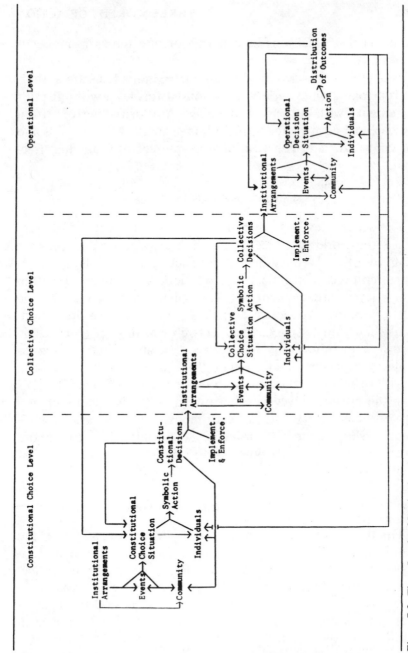

Figure 7.2   Three Levels of Institutional Analysis

207

contingencies. Decisions in a market or in a tennis game occur at this level.

In a highly organized and free society, individuals are authorized to take a wide variety of actions at this level without prior agreement with other individuals. Authority derives from institutional arrangements, including property law, business and corporate law, and constitutional guarantees of individual freedom.

The World of Collective Choice

The second level of analysis, shown in the center of Figure 7.2, is the world of collective decisions. Collective decisions are made by officials (including citizens acting as officials) to determine, enforce, continue, or alter actions authorized within institutional arrangements. Like individual strategies in the world of action, collective decisions are plans for future action. Unlike individual strategies, collective decisions are enforceable against nonconforming individuals. An individual failing to abide by a personal diet strategy, for example, may feel guilty, but no official has the power to enforce the diet plan. Officials have the power, however, to enforce a collective plan such as a city ordinance. City officials can impose sanctions against individuals who violate the ordinance. The authority to impose sanctions is a key attribute of the collective choice level of decision-making.

The World of Constitutional Choice

The third level, shown in the left section of Figure 7.2, is the world of constitutional decision-making. Constitutional decisions are collective choices about rules governing future collective decisions to authorize actions. Constitutional choices, in other words, are decisions about decision rules. Organizing an enterprise is a constitutional decision about rules to constrain future collective choices within the enterprise. But constitutional choice also continues beyond the initial organizing period, for as individuals react to consequences of earlier rules for collective decision-making, participants may change the rules to improve the result.

While components of the framework are similar across the three levels of analysis, attributes may vary in importance from one level to another. The framework, however, shows the potential for institutional models to explain a broad range of situations, with institutional arrangements linking each level of decision-making to the next level. Constitutional decisions establish institutional arrangements and their enforcement for collective choice. Collective decisions, in turn, establish institutional arrangements and their enforcement for individual action.

DIFFERENCES AMONG THE LEVELS
OF DECISION-MAKING

The decision at the operational level differs fundamentally from the decisions at the other two levels. But the ease with which scholars have adapted similar analytical models to all three levels of decision-making have masked this difference. *The operational level is the only level of analysis where an action in the physical world flows directly from a decision.* Individuals do not act directly upon decisions in the worlds of collective or constitutional choice. Decision makers, instead, select symbols conveying information about preferred future actions.

In the world of collective choice, decision makers select among proposals to authorize future actions or select among candidates for official positions in future collective choice situations. But the only immediate results from the decisions are symbolic expressions, like votes. Aggregated votes, then, produce a collective decision about a plan for future action or about the selection of public officials. The individuals making the collective decisions sometimes also undertake the actions authorized by the collective decision, but frequently, the collective decision makers are different individuals from those taking the authorized action. Legislators, for example, make collective decisions governing actions by administrative employees.

Another difference between the operational level and the other two levels of decision-making is the role of implementation and enforcement. Figure 7.2 shows this difference by including a working part for implementation and enforcement in the constitutional and collective choice level but not in the operational level. Constitutional and collective decisions must be implemented and enforced to ensure controls over the world of action, although analysts frequently assume that this aspect of political economy occurs automatically. Studies such as those by Pressman and Wildavsky (1973) illustrate the folly of such assumptions.

Our framework also calls attention to the distinction between constitutional and collective decision-making. This is another point of confusion in political-economic literature. Writers frequently call both kinds of decisions "politics," missing the point that constitutional choices precede and constrain collective choices. Calling both kinds of decisions by the same name brings us, as Buchanan (1977: 71) asserts, "deep in the cardinal sin of using the same word, politics, to mean two quite different things, and indeed this double use has been one of the major sources of modern confusion."

Our tennis example illustrates the distinctions and the relationships among the three levels of analysis. The Intercollegiate Tennis Association determines the rules for college tennis. The association's members make up the community at the collective choice level of analysis, and individual representatives of the association members are the decision makers. The collective decision situation describes the alternatives and the consequences regarding the selection of rules for intercollegiate tennis.

Members of the association interact and representatives individually decide upon tournament rules. Representatives confront decision situations at the collective choice level, analogous to the tennis player deciding whether to charge the net or to play the baseline at the operational level. The representative makes the decision and voices that decision according to institutional arrangements at the collective choice level. These symbolic actions by the several representatives are then aggregated, again according to the institutional arrangement, into a collection decision. This collective decision becomes part of the rule configuration that constrains interaction among college tennis players in the future.

Imagine that the Intercollegiate Tennis Association must decide whether to raise the net by six inches for all intercollegiate tennis games after some future date. When deciding, association members will consider the makeup of the Intercollegiate Tennis Association (that is, the community), the constraint on the range of choices members can make (institutional arrangements), and the nature of the good over which the Intercollegiate Tennis Association members are interacting (the game or the event). The decision situation resulting from these three elements necessarily differs from decision situations regarding intercollegiate tennis at the operational level, because the elements shaping the decision situation change from one level to the next. The attributes of the good for example, differ between the collective choice and operational levels of analysis. A tennis game, at the operational level, may be a private means for two rivals to challenge each other. At the collective choice level, tennis extends beyond a private matter between two players to matters involving all members of the association. Tennis, at the collective choice level, becomes a joint consumption good.

FEEDBACK MECHANISM IN THE THREE WORLDS

Feedback paths at the operational level also exist at the collective choice and the constitutional choice levels. Collective decisions resulting from the aggregated individual vote increase the shared experience of the community. The shared experience affects collective decision situations on subsequent rounds of the process. The results also affect the awareness of individual decision makers, causing them to vote differently in subsequent rounds.

Feedback paths also cross the levels of analysis. The representation of the linkages can become quite complex, depending on the channel of the feedback. The feedback may be as simple as having the distribution of outcomes at the operational level change the attributes of the individual member who participates in the collective choice. On the other hand, the feedback may be complex, working through an individual who participates in the operational decision situation and later pressures other individuals at the collective choice level to alter their decisions. This individual, then, operating at a collective choice level by voting for members of the Intercollegiate Tennis Association or otherwise pressuring the members of the association, helps produce a collective decision that affects the attributes of the individual member of the association. Perhaps the combined pressure from a number of disgruntled players makes the association member more aware of the outcomes of a particular tennis rule and causes the member to vote differently in future collective choice situations regarding the troublesome rule.

The rules that govern the collective choice situation are determined at the third level of political-economy framework in the constitutional choice situation. The constitutional level determines the formal composition of the collective choice body and how the members of the body are selected. The constitutional level determines the issues that the collective choice body can address and how the body can address those issues. The constitutional level determines the relationship among the members of the collective choice body.

Individual administrators and members of athletic departments in a wide variety of colleges and universities with potential for playing intercollegiate tennis can form a body to establish an Intercollegiate Tennis Association. The members of that body have to construct the association, determining its size, how the members of the association are to be selected, the responsibilities of the association, and how the association is to function. Decisions regarding each one of these aspects about the association must be made by individuals in the constitutional body functioning in a constitutional choice situation.

That constitutional choice situation, as at other levels of analysis, is determined by the composition of the community from the colleges and universities interested in forming an Intercollegiate Tennis Association, the rules governing the interaction that will establish the Intercollegiate Tennis Association, and the good that intercollegiate tennis represents. The schools may agree that all interested schools have one vote in the constitution of the association or that the larger universities have more votes in constituting the association than the smaller colleges. The members may bar some schools from participating in the constitutional level of choice.

The good may be seen as competition among various colleges and universities, of which tennis is only one part of that competition. The schools may be interested in establishing contact and rivalry with each other in a variety of ways and see the constituting of a tennis association as a means to begin that rivalry. They foresee this rivalry and contact as eventually spilling over into other sports and into academic areas.

This view of the good, combined with the limits on the schools that can participate in the constitutional choices and the rules that govern the constitutional choice process, determines the choice situation that each individual participating in constitutional choices confronts. Change the representation by the schools from heavy influence by administrators to heavy influence by athletic departments, and the alternatives open to individual choice makers will change. Change the good from an attempt to foster contact and rivalry among the schools to an attempt to increase the fund-raising potential of the various schools, and the choice situations confronting the individual choice makers will change. Changes in these working parts of the system will reverberate through the redesign of the Intercollegiate Tennis Association, through changes in the rules governing the play of intercollegiate tennis, through changes in the decision situation that encourages charging the net to a situation that encourages playing the baseline, to less aggressive games in intercollegiate tennis.

Feedback occurs within the constitutional level of analysis, as it does within the other levels. Individuals participating in the design of institutional arrangements make a choice regarding a rule within the institutional configuration on the basis of certain levels of knowledge and awareness about the consequences of alternative votes. The aggregation of individual votes on the rule alternatives is a constitutional decision, which may be a consequence that the individual voter did not expect, given the constitutional choice situation. But having gone through the process, the individual is now more aware of the relationships among the alternatives up for vote and the likely consequences. In similar rounds in the future at the constitutional level, that individual could vote differently because of this new level of awareness.

A participant from one of the small colleges in the process of constructing the Intercollegiate Tennis Association may learn from a vote about the representation on the association that the large universities are agreeing on a united position before the vote. In the meantime, the smaller colleges entered the vote with little foreknowledge of each other's preferences and no agreement among themselves on a position to take. The result is a rule that gives the universities disproportionately heavy representation in the association. The participant from the small college may have expected that the universities would be more heavily represented, but not by as much as the actual constitutional decision allowed. On the next vote college participants may circulate proposals prior to a meeting with each other and work out a united position before the vote. On a similar issue, the individual's vote this time is different, even though the constitutional choice situation may be similar to the first situation.

Feedback also crosses from one level to the next. Figure 7.2 shows that outcomes at the operational level can feed back to the individual participating at the collective choice level and to the individual participating at the constitutional choice level. These individuals may or may not be the same individual as the one who decides at the operational level, and even when the three individuals are the same individual, the attributes that are brought to bear on the choice situation at the three levels may be very different. In effect, the individual enters the choice situations at the three levels as though the individual were three different individuals.

Figure 7.2 and this discussion purposely keep the linkages among the three levels of analysis and the feedback routes simple. The levels and their interrelationships are often very complicated. The decision situation will often be affected simultaneously by the rules of many institutional arrangements, rather than one arrangement as represented in Figures 7.1 and 7.2. The rule, for example, that a tennis player cannot shoot and kill an opposing player, because he charges the net or otherwise plays aggressively, comes from a state government rather than the Intercollegiate Tennis Association. Thus, more than one set of collective choices bears upon the decision situation at the operational level. Moreover, each set of collective choices is made within the rules of different constitutions.

Another complication is the problem of deciding where to stop adding levels to Figure 7.2. Even at the constitutional choice level, there are rules that affect the choice situation. Thus, some means of determining those rules must exist. That is, there must be a preconstitutional level and a pre-preconstitutional level. The problem is the one of infinite regress that Buchanan and Tullock (1962) speak of in *The Calculus of Consent,* when they begin their analysis at the constitutional level with the rule of unanimity.

Such complications, however, add little to the explanatory and predictive powers of the framework, only serving to make it more cumbersome. We are trying here to provide a framework to enable scholars to understand the bare bones of this approach. Once this minimal structure is understood, the analyst can proceed to add still more complexity to the framework.

CONCLUSION

In this chapter we have taken an ecumenical rather than a parochial view of a family of theories that all use the individual as a basic unit of analysis. These theories examine the effect of institutional arrangements on the decision situations in which individuals act, producing results for themselves and others. The number of variables and complex linkages involved when scholars attempt to develop and test theories of institutions has confused many pursuing the attempt as well as their readers. The schematic framework presented above develops what we consider to be the essential elements and key linkages among three levels of analysis—constitutional, collective, and operational—and within any one of these levels. It is our hope that this metatheoretical approach helps scholars to understand the working parts of theories that have the surface appearance of being totally unrelated.

Using this framework, neoclassical economics can be viewed as a particular theory focusing primarily on the world of action. The definition of the individual used is relatively narrow. The decision situation constituted by institutional arrangements, goods, and community is limited in scope and presents individuals with little real choice. Tight linkages between individual actions and group results exist and are easy to understand for participants as well as observers. Analytical methods have been successful in predicting results when real-world situations closely resemble the highly limited situations posited by the theory.

The assumptions developed in neoclassical economics about the individual are the gears that drive the analytical machine. Because of this, many have viewed the assumptions as having an independent existence of their own, unrelated to the assumptions made about the other working parts of a particular theory. Thus, considerable work in political science has adopted the narrowly defined model of the individual used in neoclassical economics as "the" definition of a rational individual, no matter what type of situation is being modeled. However, we would argue that it is the nature of the situation being modeled that produces the opportunity to model the individual in this narrow fashion. The competitive market as modeled produces highly specific information about prices sufficient for an individual to have complete information. But complete information in this case is focused on one piece of information—current market price.

We see no reason to assume that the specific model of the individual that has been so successful as part of a particular theory should be as successful an analytic device when picked up and thrust into theories attempting to explain dramatically different types of decision situations. In a legislature or an election, the number of relevant variables, the degree of direct effect on participants, the level of information, and the tightness of the linkage structure all differ substantially from a market.

As Boynton points out in Chapter 2, all theories specify relationships between some variables under well-defined conditions. The conditions of the competitive market are well specified and describe only a small segment of the decision situation one could analyze using the framework presented above. Under these conditions, analytical solutions can be derived that have nice equilibrium properties. Because of the type of institutional arrangements, goods, and community, the constituted decision situation in a competitive market can be modeled as relatively mechanistic.

Theories that apply this framework to other types of decision situations may attempt to gain analytical solutions but will frequently lose explanatory power as a result of the unreality of the assumptions needed to drive analytical solutions. To assume that individuals perform calculation processes requiring high levels of information when they are acting in uncertain environments may lead to the formulation of beautiful analytical models that are empirically irrelevant. A major question to be pursued is how institutional arrangements help to structure decision situations in complex arenas so that individuals are able to achieve productive outcomes even when we cannot derive analytic solutions. If we limit the way we model individuals and situations to those models that have been successful in explaining market behavior, we may continually fail to show how *different* institutional arrangements help fallible and less than fully informed persons to achieve relatively satisfactory outcomes.

NOTES

1. The extent of closeting institutional variables is illustrated in examining the table of contents and index of Dahl and Lindblom's major study, *Politics, Economics and Welfare* (1953). The term "institution" does not appear in any form in the contents or index. The term "law" appears in the index paired with the term "command," and two pages are cited—both of which focus on a sociological definition of the power of a leader to command the performance of a subordinate. The term "rule" is paired in the index with the term "regulation." The three pages cited all discuss bureaucratic rules and regulations as conceptualized as "red tape." It is difficult to contemplate how difficult it must have been to do a comparative study of markets, voting, and hierarchical decision mechanisms without examining self-consciously the rule systems affecting these different processes.

2. Commons (1959: 54) recognized that the predictability of behavior depended both on the willingness of participants to follow rules as ethical systems and on the probability that officials will enforce their claims to rights if remedial action was requested. He articulated both in the following way:

> Now the distinction between ethical rights and duties and legal rights and duties is the distinction between two classes of probability respecting human conduct. Legal rights and duties are none other than the probability that officials will act in a certain way respecting the claims that citizens make against each other. . . . But there is also an ethical ideal not relating directly to the state, and an ethical probability. In most of the transactions of modern society respecting the rights of property, liberty, domestic relations and so on, scarcely one transaction in a billion gets before the courts or in the hands of public officials. These ethical transactions are guided, nevertheless, to an indefinite extent, by the probabilities of official behavior, but the bulk of transactions are on an ethical level guided by ethical ideals considerably above the minimum legal probabilities of what officials will do.

3. For a classification of rules for the purpose of identifying whether the rules relate solely to (1) interactions among individuals, (2) relations of individuals to objects, or (3) relations among individuals with respect to objects, see Montias (1976: 24-25). Douglas Rae (1971) partially classified institutional rules for the purpose of asking how they might contribute to the degree of political democracy within a system.

4. Recent work in experimental economics is extremely important for the purpose of isolating the effect of specific institutional rules on the type of behavior

adopted and results produced in controlled decision situations. See Smith (1978), Coppinger et al. (1980); and Cox et al. (1981).

5. This section draws heavily on V. Ostrom and E. Ostrom (1977a). See also the discussion in Benjamin, Chapter 3 in this volume.

REFERENCES

Aristotle (1962) *The Politics.* Baltimore: Penguin.
Alchian, A. A. and H. Demsetz (1972) "Production, information costs, and economic organizations." *American Economic Review* 62, 5: 777-795.
Arrow, K. (1966) *Social Choice and Individual Values* (2nd. ed.). New York: John Wiley.
——— (1969) "The organization of economic activity: issues pertinent to the choice of market versus nonmarket allocation," in *The Analysis and Evaluation of Public Expenditures: The PPB System.* Washington, DC: U.S. Congress, Joint Economic Committee, Subcommittee on Economy in Government.
Auster, R. D. and M. Silver (1979) *The State as a Firm: Economic Forces in Political Development.* Boston: Martinus Nijhoff.
Becker, G. S. (1976) *The Economic Approach to Human Behavior.* Chicago: University of Chicago Press.
Black, D. (1958) *The Theory of Committees and Elections.* Cambridge, MA: Cambridge University Press.
Blumstein, J. (1981) "The resurgence of institutionalism." *Journal of Policy Analysis and Management* 1, 1: 129-132.
Borcherding, T. E. [ed.] (1977) *Budgets and Bureaucrats.* Durham, NC: Duke University Press.
Boulding, K. E. (1963) "Towards a pure theory of threat systems." *American Economic Review* 53, 2: 424-434.
Bowen, H. R. (1943-1944) "The interpretation of voting in the allocation of economic resources." *Quarterly Journal of Economics* 58 (November): 27-48.
Brunner, K. and W. H. Meckling (1977) "The perception of man and the conception of government." *Journal of Money, Credit and Banking* 9,1 (Pt. 1): 70-85.
Buchanan, J. M. (1970) "Public goods and public bads," pp. 51-71 in J. P. Crecine (ed.) *Financing the Metropolis.* Beverly Hills, CA: Sage Publications.
——— (1972) "Towards analysis of closed behavioral systems," in J. M. Buchanan and R. D. Tollison (eds.) *Theory of Public Choice. Political Applications of Economics.* Ann Arbor: University of Michigan Press.
——— (1975) "Individual choice in voting and the market." *Journal of Political Economy* 62, 3: 334-343.
——— (1977) *Freedom in Constitutional Contract: Perspectives of a Political Economist.* College Station: Texas A&M University Press.
——— and G. Tullock (1962) *The Calculus of Consent: Logical Foundations of Constitutional Democracy.* Ann Arbor: University of Michigan Press.
Caves, R. (1977) *American Industry: Structure, Conduct, and Performance* (4th ed.). Englewood Cliffs, NJ: Prentice-Hall.
Coase, R. H. (1937) "The nature of the firm." *Economica* (new series) 4, 16: 386-405.

Coleman, J. (1973) *The Mathematics of Collective Action.* Chicago: Aldine.

Commons, J. R. (1950) *The Economics of Collective Action.* New York: Macmillan.

――― (1959) *Legal Foundations of Capitalism.* Madison: University of Wisconsin Press.

Coppinger, V., V. L. Smith, and J. Titus (1980) "Incentives and behavior in English, Dutch, and sealed-bid auctions." *Economic Inquiry* 18 (January): 1-22.

Cox, J. C., B. Robertson, and V. L. Smith (1981) "Theory and behavior of single object auctions." Tucson: University of Arizona.

Dahl, R. A. and C. E. Lindblom (1953) *Politics, Economics, and Welfare, Planning, and Politics—Economic Systems Resolved into Basic Social Processes.* New York: Harper & Row.

Downs, A. (1957) *An Economic Theory of Democracy.* New York: Harper & Row.

――― (1967) *Inside Bureaucracy.* Boston: Little, Brown.

Elster, J. (1977) *Ulysses and the Sirens.* New York: Cambridge University Press.

Farquharson, R. (1969) *Theory of Voting.* New Haven, CT: Yale University Press.

Hamburger, H. (1979) *Games as Models of Social Phenomena.* San Francisco: Freeman.

Head, J. G. (1962) "Public goods and public policy." *Public Finance* 17, 3: 197-219.

Hirschman, A. O. (1970) *Exit, Voice, and Loyalty. Responses to Declines in Firms, Organizations, and States.* Cambridge, MA: Harvard University Press.

Hurwicz, L. (1973) "The design of mechanisms for resource allocation." *American Economic Review* 63, 2: 1-30.

Jensen, M. C. and W. H. Meckling (1976) "Theory of the firm: managerial behavior, agency costs and ownership structure." *Journal of Financial Economics* 3, 4: 305-360.

Katz, D. and R. L. Kahn (1966) *The Social Psychology of Organizations.* New York: John Wiley.

Kirzner, I. M. (1973) *Competition and Entrepreneurship.* Chicago: University of Chicago Press.

Knight, F. H. (1921) *Risk, Uncertainty, and Profit.* New York: Houghton Mifflin.

――― (1965) *Freedom and Reform.* New York: Harper Row.

Kramer, G. H. and J. Hertzberg (1975) "Formal theory," pp. 351-404 in F. L. Greenstein and N. W. Polsby (eds.) *Handbook of Political Science.* Reading, MA: Addison-Wesley.

Leibenstein, H. (1976) *Beyond Economic Man.* Cambridge, MA: Harvard University Press.

Luce, R. and H. Raiffa (1957) *Games and Decisions: An Introduction and Critical Survey.* New York: John Wiley.

March, J. G. (1978) "Bounded rationality, ambiguity, and the engineering of choice." *Bell Journal of Economics* 9, 2: 587-608.

――― and H. A. Simon (1958) *Organizations.* New York: John Wiley.

Marschak, J. (1968) "Economics of inquiring, communicating, deciding." *American Economic Review* 58 (May): 1-18.

Montias, J. M. (1976) *The Structure of Economic Systems.* New Haven, CT: Yale University Press.

Mueller, D. C. (1979) *Public Choice.* Cambridge, MA: Cambridge University Press.

Musgrave, R. A. (1959) *The Theory of Public Finance: A Study in Public Economy.* New York: McGraw-Hill.

Niskanen, W. A. (1971) *Bureaucracy and Representative Government*. Chicago: Aldine.

Olson, M. (1965) *The Logic of Collective Action: Public Goods and the Theory of Groups*. Cambridge, MA: Harvard University Press.

Ostrom, V. (1973) *The Intellectual Crisis in American Public Administration*. University: University of Alabama Press.

——— (1976) "Some paradoxes for planners: human knowledge and its limitations." pp. 243-254 in A. L. Chickering (ed.) *The Politics of Planning: A Review and Critique of Centralized Economic Planning*. San Francisco: Institute for Contemporary Studies.

——— (1980) "Artisanship and artifact." *Public Administration Review* 40, 4: 309-317.

——— (forthcoming) *The Political Theory of a Compound Republic* (rev. ed.). New Brunswick, NJ: Transaction.

——— and T. Hennessey (1975) *Conjectures of Institutional Analysis and Design: An Inquiry into Principles of Human Governnance*. Bloomington: Indiana University, Workshop in Political Theory and Policy Analysis.

Ostrom, V. and E. Ostrom (1977a) "Public goods and public choices, pp. 7-49 in E. S. Savas (ed.) *Alternatives for Delivering Public Services. Toward Improved Performance*. Boulder, CO: Westview.

——— (1977b) "A theory for institutional analysis of common pool problems," pp. 157-172 in G. Hardin and J. Baden (eds.) *Managing the Commons*. San Francisco: Freeman.

Parks, R. B. et al. (1981) "Consumers as coproducers of public services: some economic and institutional considerations." *Policy Studies Journal* 9, 7: 1001-1011.

Popper, K. R. (1967) "La rationalité et le statut du principle de rationalité," pp. 145-150 in E. M. Classen (ed.) *Les Foundements Philosophiques des Systémes Economiques: Textes de Jacques Rueff et Essais Rediges en son Monneur 23 aout 1966*. Paris: Payot.

Pressman, J. L. and A. B. Wildavsky (1973) *Implementation: How Great Expectations in Washington Are Dashed in Oakland*. Berkeley: University of California Press.

Rae, D. W. (1971) "Political democracy as a property of political institutions." *American Political Science Review* 65, 1: 111-119.

Riker, W. H. (1980) "Implications from the disequilibrium of majority rule for the study of institutions." *American Political Science Review* 74, 2: 432-445.

——— and P. C. Ordeshook (1973) *An Introduction to Positive Political Theory*. Englewood Cliffs, NJ: Prentice-Hall.

Ross, S. A. (1973) "The economic theory of agencies: the principal's problem." *American Economic Review* 63, 2: 134-139.

Samuelson, P. A. (1954) "The pure theory of public expenditure." *Review of Economics and Statistics* 36 (November): 387-389.

——— (1955) "Diagrammatic exposition of a theory of public expenditure." *Review of Economics and Statistics* 37, 4: 350-356.

Savas, E. S. (1978) "The institutional structure of local government services: a conceptual model." *Public Administration Review* 38, 5: 412-419.

Schelling, T. C. (1978) *Micromotives and Macrobehavior*. New York: Norton.

Sen, A. K. (1970) *Collective Choice and Social Welfare*. San Francisco: Holden-Day.

Shepsle, K. A. (1974) "Theories of collective choice," pp. 1-87 in C. P. Cotter (ed.) *Political Science Annual* (Vol. 5). Indianapolis: Bobbs-Merrill.

——— (1979) "Institutional arrangements and equilibrium in multidimensional voting models." *American Journal of Political Science* 23: 27-59.

——— and B. R. Weingast (1981) "Political preferences for the pork barrel: a generalization." *American Journal of Political Science* 25, 1: 96-111.

Shubik, M. (1959) *Strategy and Market Structure: Competition, Oligopoly, and the Theory of Games*. New York: John Wiley.

——— (1975) "Oligopoly theory, communication, and information." *American Economic Review* 65 (May): 280-283.

Simon, H. A. (1957) *Models of Man: Social and Rational*. New York: John Wiley.

——— (1972) "Theories of bounded rationality," in C. McGuire and R. Radner (eds.) *Decision and Organization*. Amsterdam: Elsevier North Holland.

——— (1978) "Rationality as process and as product of thought." *American Economic Review* 68, 2: 1-16.

Simon, H. A. (1981) *The Sciences of the Artificial* (2nd ed.). Cambridge, MA: MIT Press.

Smith, V. L. (1976) "Experimental economics: induced value theory." *American Economic Review* 66 (May): 274-279.

——— (1978) "Experimental mechanisms for public choice," pp. 323-355 in P. C. Ordeshook (ed.) *Game Theory and Political Science*. New York: New York University Press.

Taylor, M. (1976) *Anarchy and Cooperation*. New York: John Wiley.

Thaler, R. H. and H. M. Sheffrin (1981) "A theory of self-control." *Journal of Political Economy* 89, 2: 392-406.

Tullock, G. (1965) *The Politics of Bureaucracy*. Washington, DC: Public Affairs Press.

Williamson, O. E. (1975) *Markets and Hierarchies: Analysis and Anti-Trust Implications. A Study in the Economics of Internal Organizations*. New York: Macmillan.

About the Authors

BRIAN BARRY is Distinguished Service Professor of Political Science and Philosophy at the University of Chicago. His undergraduate degree and doctorate were gained at the University of Oxford, where he later spent six years as a Fellow of Nuffield College. He was the founding editor of the *British Journal of Political Science* and is currently editor of *Ethics: An International Journal of Social, Political and Legal Philosophy.* His books include *Political Argument* (London: Routledge & Kegan Paul, 1965); *Sociologists, Economists and Democracy* (1970; reprinted by the University of Chicago Press, 1978); and *The Liberal Theory of Justice: A Critical Examination of the Principal Doctrines in A Theory of Justice by John Rawls* (Oxford: Clarendon Press, 1973).

ROGER BENJAMIN is Professor of Political Science at the University of Minnesota. His most recent books are *The Limits of Politics, Collective Goods and Political Change In Postindustrial Societies* (Chicago: University of Chicago Press, 1980) and *Tradition and Change in Postindustrial Japan: The Role of Political Parties* (with Kan Ori; New York: Praeger, 1981). He has published numerous articles on the subjects of comparative political economy and political change.

G. R. BOYNTON received his Ph.D. from the University of North Carolina in 1964, and has been at the University of Iowa since. He had been Director of the Laboratory for Political Research and Departmental Executive Officer. He was the Program Director of Political Science at the National Science

223

Foundation from 1972 through 1974. His most recent book is *Mathematical Thinking About Politics.*

LARRY L. KISER is Associate Professor of Economics and Public Administration and directs the Center for Social and Economic Research at Eastern Washington University. He is interested in applying economic analysis to public-sector problems. His recent research focuses on citizen production of public services and the analysis of collective goods.

J. DONALD MOON is Associate Professor of Government at Wesleyan University. He has published "The Logic of Political Inquiry" in the *Handbook of Political Science,* and essays in *Political Theory, Journal of Politics, Philosophy of the Social Sciences,* and other journals. He is currently working on problems relating to environmentalism and the legitimacy of the liberal-democratic welfare state.

ELINOR OSTROM is Chair of the Department of Political Science and Co-Director of the Workshop in Political Theory and Policy Analysis at Indiana University. Her research interests are in the study of urban service delivery and the effects of institutional arrangements on citizens, elected officials, bureau chiefs, and street-level bureaucrat behavior. She is the author of *Urban Policy Analysis: An Institutional Approach* and the editor of *The Delivery of Human Services: Outcomes of Change.*

JOHN SPRAGUE was educated at Stanford, receiving his Ph.D. in 1964. After a one-year Social Science Research Council postdoctoral fellowship, he joined the faculty of Washington University, St. Louis, in 1965, where he is now Professor of Political Science. His research has ranged from lawyers and judges through the history of electoral socialism to civil riots, and currently is focused on the influences of social and political contexts on mass behavior. For exercise, or recreation, or both, he likes to sail.